D1715822

TRUTH AND ONTOLOGY

Truth and Ontology

Trenton Merricks

CLARENDON PRESS · OXFORD

OXFORD
UNIVERSITY PRESS

Great Clarendon Street, Oxford OX2 6DP

Oxford University Press is a department of the University of Oxford.
It furthers the University's objective of excellence in research, scholarship,
and education by publishing worldwide in

Oxford New York

Auckland Cape Town Dar es Salaam Hong Kong Karachi
Kuala Lumpur Madrid Melbourne Mexico City Nairobi
New Delhi Shanghai Taipei Toronto

With offices in

Argentina Austria Brazil Chile Czech Republic France Greece
Guatemala Hungary Italy Japan Poland Portugal Singapore
South Korea Switzerland Thailand Turkey Ukraine Vietnam

Oxford is a registered trade mark of Oxford University Press
in the UK and in certain other countries

Published in the United States
by Oxford University Press Inc., New York

British Library Cataloguing in Publication Data
Data available

Library of Congress Cataloging in Publication Data
Data available

Typeset by Laserwords Private Limited, Chennai, India
Printed in Great Britain
on acid-free paper by
Biddles Ltd, King's Lynn, Norfolk

ISBN 978-0-19-920523-3

1 3 5 7 9 10 8 6 4 2

For Emily, Conor, and William

ACKNOWLEDGEMENTS

Much of this book was written during the academic year 2004–2005, while I enjoyed a fellowship from the National Endowment for the Humanities and a year's leave from the University of Virginia. The University supplied further leave during the spring of 2006. I am, of course, very grateful both to the University and to the NEH for their generous support of this project.

I presented excerpts from this book at the University of Virginia (2005), the University of Texas (2006), the State University of New York at Buffalo (2006), and the Central Division APA Symposium on Truthmakers (2006). Thanks to the audiences at those talks. Thanks also to the University of Virginia faculty and graduate students who participated in a reading group on the manuscript during the spring of 2006. More generally, thanks to everyone who made constructive suggestions, raised good objections, and answered my questions. In particular, thanks to Tal Brewer, Tom Crisp, Mitch Green, Brannon McDaniel, Becky Stangl, and Cathy Sutton. And I am especially grateful to Mike Bergmann, Jim Cargile, Harold Langsam, Matt McGrath, Mark Murphy, Josh Parsons, Mike Rea, Ted Sider, Donald Smith, and Nick Wolterstorff for extensive and extremely helpful comments on every aspect of the entire manuscript.

T. M.
Charlottesville, Virginia

CONTENTS

Contents

INTRODUCTION

That Fido is brown is true because Fido is brown. *That the Trojans were conquered* is true because the Trojans were conquered. *That hobbits do not exist* is true because hobbits do not exist. And so on. And so we might say that truth 'depends on the world'. But such 'dependence' is trivial. No one would deny it. This book considers whether, in addition to the trivial dependence just noted, there is a substantive way in which truth depends on the world or on things or on being.

A thorough exploration of whether, and how, truth depends substantively on being forces us to consider questions that, at first glance, seem to have little to do with truth. This is because, as we shall see, any account of truth's substantive dependence on being has implications for a variety of other philosophical debates. And so this book examines how theses that attempt to articulate truth's dependence on being influence—and are themselves influenced by—theories concerning, among other things, modality, time, dispositions, and the nature of truth itself.

The thesis known as *Truthmaker* is one attempt to articulate truth's dependence on being. Truthmaker says that each truth has a 'truthmaker'. That is, Truthmaker says that for each claim that is true, there is some entity that, by its mere existence, makes that claim true. Because it is an account of truth's substantive dependence on being, Truthmaker has implications for a variety of philosophical debates. Most obviously, Truthmaker is inconsistent with any philosophical theory that ends up being committed to truths that lack truthmakers.

Typical truthmaker theorists do not see a philosophical theory committed to truthmakerless truths as posing a potential challenge to Truthmaker. Instead, they automatically conclude that, since it fails to pass their Truthmaker-based litmus test, that theory must be false. These truthmaker theorists thereby treat Truthmaker more as a tool for doing philosophy—a tool for narrowing down the live options—than as a controversial bit of philosophy itself.

This book will show, however, that Truthmaker is no less a controversial philosophical theory than are the theories with which it clashes. And, more generally, this book will show that what we should say about truth's dependence on being turns on what we should say about being as much as it turns on what we should say about truth. By the end of the book, I shall have concluded that some truths simply fail to depend on being in any substantive way at all. Along the way, we shall gain new insights into the many theories that interact with Truthmaker and related theses.

But the book begins with Truthmaker. As we see in the first chapter, 'Truthmaker and *Making True*', Truthmaker purports to articulate the idea that truth depends substantively on being. And so it is primarily motivated by the intuition that truth does indeed depend substantively on being and, similarly, by the desire to rule out theories that violate that dependence. (Truthmaker is also sometimes motivated by the mistaken belief that it is identical with the correspondence theory of truth.) Chapter 1 defends a partial account of *making true*: x makes p true only if, necessarily, if both x and p exist, then p is true.

The second chapter, 'Truthmakers', argues that, if every truth has a truthmaker, then some of those truthmakers are states of affairs or, in other words, events, or Russellian facts. Moreover, some of those truthmaking states of affairs must have certain of their constituents essentially. Furthermore, if

Truthmaker is to rule out those theories typically taken to violate truth's dependence on being, it must exclude some alleged properties from truthmaking states of affairs. (Truthmaker's thus excluding some properties is one reason that it is not a metaphysically neutral litmus test for philosophical theories.) This chapter also argues that Truthmaker requires that a truth be 'about' its truthmaker.

'Negative Existentials', the next chapter, argues that Truthmaker should not be scaled back to allow truths such as *that hobbits do not exist* to lack truthmakers. And it argues that the best truthmaker for all such truths is a single totality state of affairs, even though this truthmaker is, so this chapter argues, subject to serious objections. This chapter also shows that Truthmaker implies that each true negative existential is really about the positive existence of something: namely, its truthmaker. These results, the chapter argues, are good reasons to doubt Truthmaker.

'Truth Supervenes on Being' is the name not only of Chapter 4, but also of a doctrine about truth. That doctrine says that what is true supervenes *globally* on which objects exist and which properties those objects exemplify; in other words, it says that all possible worlds alike with respect to which objects exist and which properties those objects exemplify are alike with respect to what is true.

Truth Supervenes on Being (TSB) intends to articulate the idea that truth depends on being. Thus TSB intends to be an alternative for advocates of truth's dependence on being who wish to reject Truthmaker. Moreover, it is an alternative with certain advantages. For example, TSB, unlike Truthmaker, has no untoward implications with respect to true negative existentials.

But TSB as a thesis of global supervenience fails to articulate the idea that truth depends substantively on being. And if TSB is to articulate that idea, so the bulk of this chapter argues, it must be recast to say, among other things, that what is true supervenes *locally* on (i.e., is necessitated by) which objects exist and which properties they exemplify. But once TSB is recast to articulate truth's dependence on being, it is not significantly better than Truthmaker, not even when it comes to negative existentials. In fact, this chapter shows that, thus recast, TSB may not really differ from Truthmaker at all.

As already noted, Chapter 4 argues that TSB must be recast if it is to articulate the idea that truth depends substantively on being. Those same arguments imply, moreover, that any adequate articulation of that idea must amount to the recast TSB or to Truthmaker. They imply, as a result, that to undermine both Truthmaker and TSB is to undermine the idea that each and every truth depends (non-trivially) on being.

As we have just seen, the first four chapters focus primarily on articulating the idea that truth depends on being in a substantive way, in a way that goes beyond the trivial and innocuous 'dependence' articulated by claims such as '*that hobbits do not exist* is true because hobbits do not exist'. Starting with Chapter 5, the book turns to other philosophical debates. As we shall see, Truthmaker and TSB have implications for each of these debates. Moreover, some of these debates have implications for whether truth depends (non-trivially) on being.

Chapter 5, 'Modality', argues that neither Lewis's modal realism nor abstract worlds reductionism can satisfy Truthmaker or TSB when it comes to truths of *de re* modality. On the contrary, both Truthmaker and TSB lead straight to irreducible modal properties. Thus Truthmaker and TSB have significant implications for the nature of modality and the inventory of irreducible properties.

'Presentism' is the sixth chapter. Presentism implies that there are no merely past objects or events. *That the Trojans were conquered* is true. Given presentism, that truth seems to lack both a truthmaker and also a supervenience base of the sort required by TSB. Thus presentism appears to be—and, this chapter argues, really is—inconsistent with Truthmaker and

TSB. Rather than take this to be a reason to reject presentism, this chapter argues, we should instead see it as a reason to jettison Truthmaker and TSB.

'Subjunctive Conditionals' is a chapter concerned primarily with dispositional conditionals and counterfactuals of freedom. Among the dispositional conditionals are claims such as *if the glass had been struck, it would have shattered*. Counterfactuals of freedom include claims like *if Curley had been offered a bribe, he would have freely taken it*. This chapter argues that neither dispositional conditionals nor counterfactuals of freedom can be made acceptable in the sight of Truthmaker or TSB.

This is not a problem for these conditionals. For subjunctive conditionals are not about the mere existence of something. Nor are they about something's actually having a certain property. And so, this chapter argues, they do not need to meet the demands of Truthmaker or TSB. More generally, this chapter concludes, only truths about the mere existence of something must have truthmakers, and only truths about what properties are actually had by actually existing things must satisfy TSB. All other truths are counterexamples to the claim that every truth must depend substantively on being.

Only truths about the mere existence of something must have truthmakers. So we should say that Truthmaker is false. We should not say, instead, that Truthmaker is true but that its scope must be curtailed. We should not say this because, as we shall see in a variety of ways throughout the book, a version of (so-called) Truthmaker that is thus curtailed cannot accommodate what motivates Truthmaker in the first place. Nor, as we shall see throughout the book, can such a version accomplish the tasks that Truthmaker has been assigned. It is best to say, then, that Truthmaker is simply false, thus signalling that its motivations are misguided and its work undone. And the same goes for TSB.

The final chapter, 'Theory of Truth', begins by arguing that the correspondence theory of truth is false. But this chapter does not thereby reject 'realism' about truth. On the contrary, this chapter insists that *that the Trojans were conquered* is true if and only if the Trojans really were conquered. It insists that *that hobbits do not exist* is true if and only if hobbits really do not exist. And so on. Moreover, this chapter refutes not only the correspondence theory of truth, but also every other version of the claim that *being true* is a relation that holds between, on the one hand, primary truth-bearers and, on the other, that in virtue of which those truth-bearers are true. It defends the claim that there is a property of *being true*. And so it concludes that *being true* is a monadic (and even a primitive) property of truth-bearers.

I

TRUTHMAKER AND *MAKING TRUE*

A THING, just by existing, can make a claim true. Thus Aristotle:

[I]f there is a man, the statement whereby we say that there is a man is true, and reciprocally—since if the statement whereby we say that there is a man is true, there is a man. And whereas the true statement is in no way the cause of the actual thing's existence, the actual thing does seem in some way the cause of the statement's being true: it is because the actual thing exists or does not that the statement is called true or false. (*Categories* 14^b15–22; 1984: 22)

Some claims are true because a thing exists. Truthmaker says that this is so for every true claim. That is, Truthmaker says that for every true claim there is something or other that—just by existing—makes that claim true. In other words, Truthmaker says that every truth has a 'truthmaker'. This chapter presents the central motivations for Truthmaker and begins to explore the *making true* relation.

I. Motivating Truthmaker

Bertrand Russell endorses Truthmaker throughout *The Philosophy of Logical Atomism*, insisting that each truth is made true by a 'fact'. J. L. Austin likewise embraces Truthmaker, saying: 'When a statement is true, there is, *of course*, a state of affairs which makes it true' (1979: 123). More recently, a growing number of philosophers have been insisting that, for each truth, there is something that makes it true. These include, among many others, William P. Alston (1996: 52), Kit Fine (1982: 69), E. J. Lowe (1998: 245), C. B. Martin (see Armstrong 1989*a*), and, most adamantly and prolifically, David Armstrong (e.g., 1997 and 2004).

Truthmaker and closely related theses have been widely endorsed and nowadays seem to be gaining new momentum. Yet even Armstrong confesses: 'The truth-maker principle seems to me to be fairly obvious once attention is drawn to it, but I do not know how to argue for it further' (1989*b*: 89). Elsewhere, Armstrong follows up the claim that he has no argument for Truthmaker with: 'My hope is that philosophers of realist inclinations will be immediately attracted to the idea that a truth, any truth, should depend for its truth [on] something 'outside' it, in virtue of which it is true' (2004: 7).

Similarly, David Lewis defends a related thesis by simply assuming Truthmaker as a starting-point and then scaling it back in light of various objections (Lewis 2001). Elsewhere, Lewis just asserts without argument that Truthmaker aims to preserve something 'right and important and underappreciated. What's right, roughly speaking, is that truths must have *things* as their subject matter' (1999*a*: 206).

No one gives much of an argument for Truthmaker. Instead, Truthmaker's main support comes from something like the brute intuition that what is true depends in a non-trivial way on what there is or the world or things or being. Truthmaker's defenders then maintain that Truthmaker is the best way to articulate that dependence.[1] This is Truthmaker's primary motivation.

---

[1] Not everyone agrees that Truthmaker is the best way to articulate that dependence. Ch. 4 examines a competing articulation.

Perhaps we can better appreciate this primary motivation by approaching it indirectly. So consider:

(1) If Queen Elizabeth II had been born in seventeenth-century Japan, she would have been a samurai warrior.

Many will object that (1) is not true. Now I suppose that you could object to (1) by arguing that, had Her Britannic Majesty been born in Japan 400 years ago, she would have been a geisha, rather than a samurai. But I am confident that most who object to (1) do so because they object to all substantive claims about what the Queen would have been like, had she been born long ago in the Land of the Rising Sun.

Those who thus object might insist that nothing could *make true* any substantive claim about what HRH would have been like, had she been born in Japan in the seventeenth century. Therefore, they conclude, neither (1) nor any other such claim is true. This argument presupposes that a truth must be 'made true' by something. And so those who find this argument against (1) compelling should support something like Truthmaker.

I do not know of any philosopher who endorses (1). But Armstrong, Lewis, and Martin object that some do endorse other claims that are not made true by being (see Lewis 1999*a*: 207). That is, they object that some philosophers cheat by violating something like Truthmaker. Indeed, Theodore Sider goes so far as to say that catching these cheaters is the whole point of Truthmaker (2001: 40). (Later chapters examine a variety of alleged cheaters.) And insofar as we think that those who violate something like Truthmaker really are cheating, we should endorse Truthmaker or some similar claim.

'Catch the cheaters' is not really a second motivation for Truthmaker, to be added to the primary motivation already noted.[2] It is, instead, that primary motivation seen in a different

---

[2] I first heard the slogan 'Catch the cheaters' in a talk by Sider.

light. For that primary motivation, which is the idea or intuition or insight that truth depends in a substantive way on what exists, is not consistent with every possible claim. As a result, there are theories that violate truth's supposed non-trivial dependence on being. Defenders of these theories are the cheaters. That is, they 'cheat' only because they defend theories inconsistent with truth's supposed non-trivial dependence on being. So opposition to cheaters and the idea that truth depends substantively on being are two sides of a single coin.

Truthmaker does not require that each truth have just one truthmaker or each truthmaker just one truth. For example, Truthmaker allows that Aristotle himself made it true not only that Aristotle exists, but also that a human exists. And Truthmaker allows that *that a human exists* was made true not only by Aristotle, but also by Plato. Along similar lines, Truthmaker does not say that truthmakers must somehow 'mirror the structure' of what they make true. For example, although it makes no sense to say that Aristotle was 'disjunctive', he made it true that either Aristotle exists or a kangaroo exists.

Suppose, somewhat controversially, that a truth can 'correspond' to something that does not mirror its structure. More to the point, suppose that each truth does indeed correspond to something, which something is thereby that truth's truthmaker. This suggests a connection between Truthmaker and the 'correspondence theory of truth'. In fact, some philosophers take Truthmaker just to be the correspondence theory. Here is John Bigelow: 'The hallowed path from language to universals has been by way of the *correspondence theory of truth*: the doctrine that whenever something is true, there must be something in the world which makes it true. I will call this the Truthmaker axiom' (1988: 122).

David Armstrong (1997: 128–31; 2000: 150; 2004: 16–17), George Molnar (2000: 85), and Alex Oliver (1996: 69) also identify Truthmaker with the correspondence theory. The best reason for thinking they are right is that familiar questions about the correspondence theory seem to be equivalent to familiar questions about Truthmaker. Compare: 'What is the *corresponding to* relation?' and 'What is the *making true* relation?' Or: 'To what do negative existential truths (e.g., *that hobbits do not exist*) correspond?' and 'What are the truthmakers for negative existential truths?'

So suppose, just for the sake of argument, that the correspondence theory is Truthmaker by another name. (But it is not; see §IV and Ch. 2, §IV.) Then to take the correspondence theory as a premiss and Truthmaker as a conclusion is to beg the question. So there is no good argument from the correspondence theory to Truthmaker. Nevertheless, the correspondence theory might be a particularly effective way to express the intuition that truth depends on being, an intuition that Truthmaker purports to clarify. Now we are back to the primary motivation for Truthmaker: the intuition that truth depends on being—and so to violate this dependence is to cheat.

II. Necessitarianism and Conditional Necessitarianism

Necessitarianism says that a truthmaker necessitates that which it makes true. That is, necessitarianism says that, for all x and all p, x is a truthmaker for p only if x's mere existence is metaphysically sufficient for p's truth. Necessitarianism's defenders include David Armstrong (2003: 12; 2004: 6–7), Kit Fine (1982: 69), John F. Fox (1987: 189), George Molnar (2000: 84), and Barry Smith (1999: 276). Understood as a necessary condition for *making true*, necessitarianism is now truthmaker orthodoxy.[3]

This section, along with the section that follows, considers how to formulate (or reformulate) necessitarianism, the

---

[3] There are heretics. Consider Bertrand Russell. He was a truthmaker theorist whose views on modality guarantee that he would have rejected necessitarianism (see Russell 1985: 96–7).

implications of necessitarianism, and what motivates necessitarianism in the first place. This will involve a lot of detail about what, at times, might seem like fairly narrow and somewhat technical issues. But these details must be addressed, since only by fully understanding necessitarianism can we hope to understand Truthmaker itself. For necessitarianism offers (by far) the least controversial necessary condition for *making true*, the relation at the heart of Truthmaker.

In fact, necessitarianism is the only widely endorsed claim among truthmaker theorists that begins to take Truthmaker from a rough idea—the idea that every truth is 'made true' by something—to a clearly formulated thesis. Moreover, as we shall see in later chapters, truthmaker theorists actually charge a view with cheating just in case that view is committed to truths that are not necessitated by what exists. Without necessitarianism, the cheater-catching business, as it has actually been run, is bankrupt.

Our examination of necessitarianism begins with a look at one of its apparent implications, an implication regarding the primary bearers of truth. Truthmaker itself seems to be neutral with respect to those primary bearers. *Qua* truthmaker theorist, so it seems, one could take them to be abstract propositions or beliefs or sentence tokens or what have you. But if necessitarianism really is part and parcel of Truthmaker, Truthmaker arguably delivers a direct argument for abstract propositions.[4]

That argument begins with:

(2) At least one electron exists.

When it comes to truthmakers for (2), we have an embarrassment of riches. Each and every electron does the trick. Thus electron E does the trick. Given necessitarianism, truthmakers

---

[4] I shall say that propositions are 'abstract' if they have no spatial location and cannot be identified with sentences (or other linguistic items) or beliefs. And I shall assume that abstract propositions exist necessarily.

necessitate their respective truths. So, in every world in which E exists, (2) is true.[5]

(2) is true in every world in which E exists. So (2) is true in W, which contains only E (and whatever E necessitates). W is bereft of language and believers. So, in W, (2) itself is neither a linguistic item nor a belief. It seems that that truth could only be an abstract proposition. In this way, Truthmaker combined with necessitarianism seems to lead directly to abstract propositions.

This sort of argument, which relies on necessitarianism, has vexed some truthmaker theorists.[6] So it would be nice to avoid it altogether. Happily, we can offer a substitute for necessitarianism that undermines this argument, even while accommodating what motivates necessitarianism.

Let *conditional necessitarianism* be the denial of necessitarianism conjoined with the claim that, for all x and p, if x is a truthmaker for p, then, necessarily, if both x and p exist, then p is true.[7] The conditional necessitarian can say that while E is

---

[5] I assume that electrons are *essentially* electrons. (If E is possibly a proton, then it is possible for E to exist but (2) be false.) Those who reject this assumption can replace (2) with, for example, *that at least one thing that is possibly an electron exists*.

[6] David Armstrong endorses 'naturalism', which he takes to be the thesis that 'the world, the totality of entities, is nothing more than the spacetime system' (1997: 5). And he says: 'no Naturalist can be happy with a realm of [abstract] propositions' (1997: 131). But Armstrong also says:

Notice that Necessitarianism seems to require that we take truths as propositions rather than as beliefs, statements, and such. Truthmakers, entities in the world, can hardly necessitate beliefs and statements about these entities, generally at least. What are propositions, then? I think that they are the *intentional objects* of actual or possible beliefs, statements and so on. I hope to give a naturalist, empiricist and, to a degree, deflationary account of intentional objects. All this, however, must be left aside here. (2003: 12)

In a more recent work, Armstrong says that propositions cannot be actual intentional objects, since there are worlds with propositions but no intentional objects. Thus he says, 'propositions taken as *possible* intentional objects are the only things that truthmakers can actually *necessitate*' (2004: 16).

[7] Conditional necessitarianism is equivalent to the claim that if x is a truthmaker for p, then it is impossible that x exist and p have a truth-value other than true (or

a truthmaker for (2), E would not make (2) true in a world in which E alone (and all that E alone necessitates) exists. For in that world neither (2) nor any other truth-bearer would exist to be made true.

It is easy to see that conditional necessitarianism undermines the above argument for abstract propositions. What is not yet clear is that conditional necessitarianism accommodates what motivates necessitarianism. For we have yet to examine those motivations. Let us start our examination with this from Armstrong's *Truth and Truthmakers*:

But what is the argument for saying that a truthmaker must necessitate a truth it is truthmaker for? Here is an argument by *reductio*. Suppose that a suggested truthmaker T for a certain truth p fails to necessitate that truth. There will then be at least the possibility that T should exist and yet the proposition p not be true. This strongly suggests that there ought to be some further condition that must be satisfied in order for p to be true. [Let this condition be] the existence of a further entity, U … [Then] T + U would appear to be the true and necessitating truthmaker for p. (2004: 6–7; see also Armstrong 1997: 115–16; Bigelow 1988: 126; and Molnar 2000: 84)[8]

Consider a putative truthmaker T for a proposition p. Suppose that T fails to necessitate p's truth. Then, Armstrong assumes,

lack a truth-value altogether). Armstrong endorses something close to conditional necessitarianism when he says: 'if a certain truthmaker makes a certain truth true, then there is no alternative world where that truthmaker exists but that truth is a false proposition' (1997: 115). Oddly, Armstrong identifies this thesis with necessitarianism.

[8] In fact, Armstrong's argument is a bit more complicated than this. He says:

This [further] condition must either be the existence of a further entity, U, or a further truth, q. In the first of these cases, T + U would appear to be the true and necessitating truthmaker for p … In the second case, q either has a truthmaker, V, or it does not. Given that q has a truthmaker, then the T + U case is reproduced. Suppose q lacks a truthmaker, then there are truths without truthmakers. (2004: 7)

I do not think that this complication involving q makes a fundamental difference to Armstrong's argument. For, as Armstrong himself says, assuming that q has a truthmaker, 'the T + U case is reproduced'.

T can be combined with some U to yield an entity whose existence is sufficient for p's truth, which new entity is p's *bona fide* truthmaker. Thus Armstrong assumes that for any true p, there is always some entity (such as $T + U$) that is suitable for making p true and whose mere existence necessitates p's truth. This assumption is a poor premiss in an argument for necessitarianism, since only someone already committed to necessitarianism would find that assumption attractive.

Armstrong's comments do, however, inspire a more persuasive argument. Suppose there are two 'contenders' to be the truthmaker for p: $T + U$, which necessitates p, and T alone, which does not. Even those on the fence about truthmaker necessitarianism might agree that, everything else being equal, $T + U$, in virtue of necessitating p, has a better claim to making p true than does T. We should ask why $T + U$, in virtue of necessitating p, has the better claim. One plausible answer is that such necessitation is at least partly constitutive of *making true*, which would imply necessitarianism.

Those who deny that p is an abstract proposition might balk at supposing that $T + U$ really could necessitate p. But they will allow $T + U$ to conditionally necessitate p. And I think it is plausible that if $T + U$ conditionally necessitates p, but T does not, then $T + U$ has a leg up on T with respect to being p's truthmaker. This can lead us to conclude that *conditional* necessitation is at least partly constitutive of *making true*. This argument for conditional necessitarianism seems to be no less compelling than the previous argument for necessitarianism. Moreover, this argument seems to accommodate what intuitively motivates that previous argument.

Here is another argument for necessitarianism. Recall:

(2) At least one electron exists.

Electron E's making (2) true is a paradigm case of truthmaking. And surely—so this argument goes—E necessitates (2). For suppose, for *reductio*, that it did not. That is, suppose that, possibly, E exists and (2) fails to be true. This implies that, possibly, E exists and (2) is false. But that implication is absurd; it is absurd to say both that an electron exists and also that it is false that at least one electron exists. So E necessitates (2). And, given that E's making (2) true is a paradigmatic case of truthmaking, the result here generalizes. Therefore, necessitarianism is true.

Those who do not already accept the existence of abstract propositions can resist the above *reductio*. For suppose that (2) is not an abstract proposition. Suppose that (2) exists contingently. This suggests that, possibly, E exists and (2) does not. Suppose that is indeed possible. If (2) does not exist, then (2) has no properties, and so no truth-value. So we can now conclude that, possibly, E exists and (2) is neither true nor false. In this way, those who deny that (2) is an abstract proposition can reject as invalid the above argument's move from 'possibly, E exists and (2) fails to be true' to 'possibly, E exists and (2) is false'.

The above argument by *reductio* should persuade only those already committed to abstract propositions. So that argument fails. Nevertheless, there is something to be learned from that argument. It is that whether or not we are initially inclined to think that truth-bearers exist necessarily, we should all agree that necessarily, if *both* E *and (2) exist*, then (2) is true.[9] And this is of course what conditional necessitarianism demands. So I think that truthmaker theorists ought to reject straight necessitarianism only if they embrace conditional necessitarianism. For truthmaker theorists should say that every truth stands to something or other in the way that (2) stands to E.

If there are abstract propositions, conditional necessitarianism collapses into straight necessitarianism. (*If* x *and* p *exist*

---

[9] Suppose you take the primary truth-bearers to be sentence tokens. Arguably, sentence tokens have their meanings contingently. So you may want to say: if E exists and (2) exists and (2) means that E exists, then (2) is true. I'll ignore this complication in what follows.

ends up collapsing, since *p* exists of necessity, into *if* x *exists*.)
On the other hand, if there are no abstract propositions, conditional necessitarianism is the better option, since straight
necessitarianism is arguably committed to such propositions.

In what follows, I shall not make much of the difference
between necessitarianism and conditional necessitarianism.
Nor do the arguments that follow usually turn on the nature
of the primary bearers of truth. But, for what it is worth, I shall
be thinking of truths as true abstract propositions, and shall
often refer to them with italicized that-clauses.

III. Truthmaker and *de re* Modality

Necessitarianism says that, for all *x* and all *p*, if *x* makes *p*
true, it is not possible that *x* exist and *p* fail to be true. It
says, in other words, that if *x* is a truthmaker for *p*, then
x is *essentially* such that *p* is true. Something similar goes
for conditional necessitarianism. So Truthmaker, given either
version of necessitarianism, is committed to *de re* modality.

John Bigelow's account of the necessitation involved in
truthmaking parts ways with both varieties of necessitarianism.
For Bigelow's account invokes only *de dicto* modality. Bigelow
says: 'I suppose that entailment is to be a relation between
propositions (whatever they are). Truthmaker should not be
construed as saying that an *object* entails a truth; rather, it
requires that the proposition *that the object exists* entails the
truth in question' (Bigelow 1988: 126). Bigelow agrees with
other truthmaker theorists that an object can be a truthmaker.
And he agrees with necessitarianism that an object's existence
somehow necessitates any claim that it makes true. But he
glosses the relevant necessitation in terms of entailment: an
object *O* thus necessitates *p* if and only if *that O exists* entails *p*.[10]

---

[10] Bigelow also suggests that truthmaker necessitarianism says that an object
entails a truth. But necessitarianism does not say this. Necessitarianism says,

There are three reasons that Bigelow's account of the necessitation involved in truthmaking should not supplant *de re* necessitation by truthmakers. (I have no objection to what Bigelow says, qualified as suggested by Fox below, if taken merely as a corollary of *de re* necessitation.) These three reasons will not only reveal problems with Bigelow's approach, but will also reinforce Truthmaker's commitment to *de re* modality, which is of particular importance later in the book (Ch. 5, §IV).

First, Aristotle was a truthmaker for *that Aristotle exists.* This means that, in some sense, Aristotle necessitated *that Aristotle exists.* Bigelow would reduce the necessitation here to the logical triviality that *that Aristotle exists* entails *that Aristotle exists.* No one denies that triviality. But the idea that Aristotle necessitated a claim that he made true is supposed to be substantive, something one could at least in principle deny. So Bigelow's claim about entailment does not capture all that there is to a truthmaker's necessitating that which it makes true.

Here is a second objection to Bigelow. The relation of *making true* holds between each truthmaker and that which it makes true. The relation of *making true* often relates an object and a claim. But the only necessitation that Bigelow recognizes in the neighbourhood of truthmaking is entailment. That sort of necessitation cannot relate an object and a claim. So that sort of necessitation cannot be an ingredient in *making true.* So Bigelow's remarks about entailment are not aimed at elucidating the *making true* relation. He has changed the subject on us.

Look at this second objection this way. Truthmaker is supposed to articulate the idea that truth depends on being. The chunk of being on which a truth depends—its truthmaker—is not typically a proposition at all. For example, return to Aristotle and *that Aristotle exists.* The truth of the latter supposedly somehow depended on the former. We do nothing to articulate

instead, only that if an object makes *p* true, then that object is essentially such that *p* is true.

the dependence of the truth of this claim on that person by saying that *that Aristotle exists* entails *that Aristotle exists*. Again, Bigelow has changed the subject on us.

My third objection to Bigelow's account starts with the observation that *that the smartest man living in Greece exists* entails *that someone lives in Greece*. And so Bigelow's account implies that the smartest man living in Greece necessitates *that someone lives in Greece*. Suppose that Aristotle was the smartest man living in Greece. Then Bigelow's account implies that Aristotle necessitated *that someone lives in Greece*. But Bigelow has led us astray. For the existence of Aristotle is consistent with Greece's being uninhabited, and so consistent with the falsity of *that someone lives in Greece*. Thus Aristotle did not necessitate *that someone lives in Greece*.

We could tweak Bigelow's account to avoid this third objection by following John F. Fox: ' ... *a*'s existing necessitates that p just when '*a* exists' entails that p. ... nothing hangs on the way *a* is named or described; the necessity intended is *de re*, not *de dicto*. So truthmaker is essentialist in Quine's sense' (Fox 1987: 189; see also Sider 2003: 182–3). Suppose that '*T*' directly refers to *T*. Let *q* be the proposition expressed by '*T* exists'. Then we could say that *T* necessitates whatever is entailed by *q*. This suggests a restriction of Bigelow's formula that avoids the unacceptable result that Aristotle necessitated *that someone lives in Greece*.

But this is all needlessly roundabout. For, as Fox notes, this roundabout approach invokes *de re* modality. And once truthmaker theorists are committed to *de re* modality, they might as well revert to necessitarianism (or to conditional necessitarianism): for all *x* and all *p*, *x* makes *p* true only if, necessarily, if *x* exists (and *p* exists) then *p* is true.[11] Moreover, necessitarianism

---

[11] Immediately following the passage quoted above, Fox (1987: 189) says: 'So it can be reformulated thus: If *p*, then some *x* exists such that *x*'s existing necessitates that *p*.'

(straight or conditional) allows Aristotle's necessitation of *that Aristotle exists* to have been more than a logical triviality. Bigelow's account, even when tweaked *à la* Fox, does not allow this. Finally, and again unlike Bigelow's account even when tweaked, necessitarianism allows a truthmaker itself to necessitate that which it makes true, thus permitting *making true* to be at least partly a matter of some sort of necessitation.

This last point is particularly important. Truthmaker just is the thesis that for each truth there is some entity x that stands in the *making true* relation to that truth. Unless we say something about the analysis of *making true*—as both kinds of necessitarianism do and as Bigelow's account does not—we have hardly any content to Truthmaker itself. A nearly empty version of Truthmaker neither articulates truth's dependence on being nor effectively catches cheaters. So, for this reason, as well as for the other reasons found in this and the preceding section, I shall proceed on the standard assumption that, according to Truthmaker, *de re* necessitation (or *de re* conditional necessitation) is at least one ingredient of *making true*.

IV. Truthmaker and the Correspondence Theory

It is hard to say anything entirely uncontroversial about the correspondence theory of truth. But here is my best shot: a necessary condition for being the correspondence theory of truth is being a *theory of truth*. That is, the correspondence theory must, at the very least, offer an analysis of *being true*. This necessary condition is all we need to refute those who say that Truthmaker is one and the same as the correspondence theory.

Consider again:

(1) If Queen Elizabeth II had been born in seventeenth-century Japan, she would have been a samurai warrior.

Truthmaker says that (1) is true only if some entity or other exists that makes (1) true. Thus Truthmaker says that (1) has a certain ontological commitment. And Truthmaker purports to reveal (1) to be not true if this commitment is not met.

More generally, Truthmaker says that every claim has ontological commitments of a certain sort. And Truthmaker catches cheaters who fail to meet those ontological commitments. But none of these claims about ontological commitment amount to—or even look remotely like—a theory of the nature of truth (see Bigelow 1988: 127; McGrath 1997: 88–9; Beebee and Dodd 2005: 13–14). Because Truthmaker offers no analysis of *being true*, Truthmaker is not the correspondence theory of truth.

There is a second reason to distinguish Truthmaker from the correspondence theory. For starters, recall that an entity's necessitating a proposition just is that entity's being essentially such that that proposition *is true*. Therefore this sort of necessitation is analysed in terms of, among other things, *being true*. (The same goes for conditional necessitation.) As we saw above, *making true* itself is at least partly analysed in terms of this sort of necessitation. Thus *making true* itself is analysed, in part, in terms of *being true*. Therefore, *being true* cannot be analysed in terms of *making true*, lest that analysis be viciously circular.

Truth cannot be analysed in terms of *making true*. But correspondence theorists say that truth is analysed in terms of *corresponding to*. So correspondence theorists must insist that *making true* is not one and the same thing as *corresponding to*. Suppose they are right. Then Truthmaker is not the correspondence theory of truth. For the identity of *making true* with *corresponding to* is essential to the idea that Truthmaker just is the correspondence theory by another name.

We have seen that one common motivation for Truthmaker—that Truthmaker is one and the same as the correspondence theory (§I)—is simply mistaken. Moreover, as we shall see in the next chapter (Ch. 2, §IV), even the weaker claim that the correspondence theory entails Truthmaker is false. Besides, even if the correspondence theory did entail Truth-maker, that would not show that Truthmaker is correct. For, as we shall see in Chapter 8 (§I), the correspondence theory of truth is false.

2

TRUTHMAKERS

THIS chapter defends the following: Truthmaker requires states of affairs, among other things, to serve as truthmakers; truthmaking states of affairs have certain of their constituents essentially; a truth is 'about' its truthmaker; and some properties are not fit to be the constituents of truthmaking states of affairs.

In combination, this chapter's conclusions present a clear picture of what truthmakers must be like. In other words, they present a clear picture of the sorts of entities to which Truthmaker is committed. Moreover, the conclusion that a truth is 'about' its truthmaker implies that there is more to the relation of *making true* than just necessitation.

I. States of Affairs as Truthmakers

Some truthmakers are humdrum and uncontroversial. Consider Fido the dog. Fido is a truthmaker for *that Fido exists*. But not all alleged truthmakers are as pedestrian as Fido. Suppose that Fido is brown. Then the following is true:

(1) Fido is brown.

Fido is contingently brown. He could have been black. Suppose he had been. Then Fido would have existed, but (1) would have

been false. So Fido does not even conditionally necessitate that
(1) is true. So Fido is not a truthmaker for (1).

Perhaps Truthmaker should permit 'joint truthmakers'.
That is, perhaps Truthmaker should say that each truth is
made true by some thing *or things*. If so, then Truthmaker
allows that there are some truths such that, for each of those
truths, there is nothing that, simply by existing, necessitates
that truth. But Truthmaker then insists that, for each of those
truths, there are some things such that, necessarily, if all of
them exist, then that truth is true. With this in mind, one might
suggest that (1)'s joint truthmakers are Fido and the property
of *being brown*. But that will not work. For it is possible for
both Fido and that property to exist even if the former fails to
exemplify the latter, even if (1) is false.

David Armstrong would say that the truthmaker for (1) is a
state of affairs. This state of affairs is not supposed to be an
abstract entity that exists necessarily, whether or not it 'obtains'.
For Armstrong's states of affairs are not the 'states of affairs'
of Alvin Plantinga (1974) or Roderick Chisholm (1976). Instead,
Armstrong's states of affairs are complex entities constituted
by objects and properties.

As Armstrong (1997: 5) explicitly notes, his states of affairs
just are Bertrand Russell's facts. Armstrong takes an object's
exemplifying a property to be a paradigmatic state of affairs.
Similarly, Russell tells us: 'The simplest imaginable facts are
those which consist in the possession of a quality by some
particular thing' (1985: 59; see also Russell 1907: 45; 1919: 1–6).
One thing's being related to another thing is an example of a
more complex fact or state of affairs.

Armstrong's states of affairs and Russell's facts are also
events, at least given one very familiar way of understanding
events. Thus Russell's *The Philosophy of Logical Atomism* illustrates J. M. Shorter's observation that 'the word "fact" … did
at one time fairly clearly mean (roughly) what "actual event"

means' (1962: 283).[1] In keeping with the terminology of the various authors discussed in this book, I shall use 'states of affairs', 'facts', and 'events' interchangeably.

As already noted, Armstrong would say that (1)—*that Fido is brown*—is made true by a state of affairs. Russell (1985) would agree, saying that (1) is made true by a fact. The state (of affairs) or fact or event of *Fido's being brown* is the most obvious candidate. But suppose, for the sake of argument, that that state could have had different constituents. Suppose, for example, that *Fido's being brown* could have been constituted by Fido and *being black*. If that state had been constituted by Fido and *being black*, then that state would have existed, and it would have been true that Fido is black. More to the point, that state would have existed and (1) would have been false. And if it is possible for that state to exist and (1) to be false, then that state is not (1)'s truthmaker.

So if *Fido's being brown* makes (1) true, then that state is essentially constituted by Fido and *being brown*. In general, if a state of affairs makes a claim true in virtue of the objects and properties that constitute that state, then that state is constituted by those objects and properties essentially.[2] Similarly, if

---

[1] Russell (1940) is an even nicer illustration, treating 'fact' and 'event' as synonymous. Nowadays, 'fact' typically means true proposition (or uncontroversially known proposition). Taking a fact to be a true abstract proposition goes back at least to Frege (1997b: 342). In 1904, Russell himself would have said that a fact was a true proposition, but only because he took true propositions to be (what we would call) events (see Ch. 8, §IV).

[2] More carefully, if a state of affairs makes p true in virtue of the objects and properties that constitute that state, then that state is not possibly constituted by other objects and properties such that, possibly, if the state is constituted by those objects and properties, then p is not true. (For example, suppose that the state of *Fido's being brown* makes *that Fido is brown or black* true. It does not follow that *being brown* is an essential constituent of that state. What follows, instead, is that that state is not possibly constituted by any property other than *being brown* or *being black*.) I shall ignore this qualification in the text. For, even given this qualification, Truthmaker has a 'controversial consequence' about the essential constituents of states of affairs, which, as we shall see, is the main point here.

some states jointly make a claim true, the constituents of those states that play a role in making that claim true are themselves essential to their respective states.

With this in mind, consider the wide variety of properties and objects that must be essential constituents of the state (or states) that is (or are) the truthmaker (or joint truthmakers) for *that Murphy's thoughts about the argument on page 627 of his dog-eared copy of* Leviathan, *which thoughts occurred from 12:15 to 12:17 on October 1, 2004, were confused at the beginning yet, through fits and starts, managed to make legitimate if moderate progress in four areas, those four areas being* ... .

Indeed, even a relatively simple truth might have an extremely complex truthmaker. Consider, once again:

(1) Fido is brown.

Some truthmaker theorists will deny that (1)'s truthmaker is the state of Fido's having the property of *being brown*, which state has Fido and *being brown* essentially. For some will insist on a 'sparse' theory of properties, according to which the only real properties are fundamental or primitive. That is, they will insist that the only real properties are not reduced to or analysed in terms of other properties. And any such philosopher will follow Armstrong (1978: 17) and deny that *being brown* exists at all, and so deny that *being brown* is a constituent of any state of affairs.

Given a sparse theory of properties, the truthmaker for (1) would have to be a complex state of affairs (or complex array of jointly truthmaking states of affairs) constituted by a wide variety of fundamental properties and their relations one to another, which essentially constitute the state (or states) involved. So the truthmaker for (1) might be no less convoluted than that for the above claim involving Murphy's thoughts.

But whatever we conclude about the exact nature of (1)'s truthmaker(s), I think we should join Armstrong and Russell and others in saying that only a state (or states) of affairs could make (1) true.[3] And so it goes for the truthmakers for many other truths. Thus we have Truthmaker's first controversial consequence: the world includes not only objects and properties, but also states of affairs.

Suppose that (1)'s truthmaker is the state of *Fido's being brown*. Then that state has both Fido and *being brown* as essential constituents. Something similar goes for other truthmaking states of affairs. Thus Truthmaker's second controversial consequence is that, for every truth involving objects, properties, and relations, there is some state (or states) constituted by those objects, properties, and relations essentially.

These controversial consequences show that Truthmaker is a substantive thesis that needs to be motivated. They also show that, at least as far as (1) is concerned, Truthmaker outstrips its primary motivation. After all, Truthmaker agrees that if (1) is

---

[3] Armstrong's principal argument for the existence of states of affairs is that they are needed for truthmaking (see, e.g., Armstrong 1997: 116–19; but see also Armstrong 2004: 48–9). Kevin Mulligan, Peter Simons, and Barry Smith (1984) make do with tropes or individual property instances in place of states of affairs. They would say that the trope of *Fido's brownness*, by its mere existence, guarantees (1)'s truth. But I shall focus on Russell's and Armstrong's approach to truthmaking. Their approach has been the more influential, perhaps because states of affairs or events are less controversial than tropes. (And even Mulligan, Simons, and Smith (1984: 295–6) slide between tropes and states of affairs in their account of truthmakers.)

Besides, my arguments regarding states of affairs as truthmakers can always be adapted to tropes. For example, this section will point out that Truthmaker has a controversial ontological implication and a controversial modal commitment; and it will say that this implies that Truthmaker outstrips its primary motivation. That point is made with states of affairs. But the same point could be made with tropes: if Truthmaker relied on tropes, it would imply, first, that tropes exist and, second, that they are essentially tropes of the entity of which they are actually tropes. (If *Fido's brownness* could be the brownness of Spot, then the mere existence of that trope would not necessitate the truth of *that Fido is brown*; see Armstrong 1989*b*: 117–18.) Here is another example. §IV argues that Truthmaker must say that some (alleged) properties may not constitute truthmaking states of affairs. That argument can easily be adapted to show that Truthmaker must deny a truthmaking role to certain (alleged) tropes.

true, then Fido exists and is brown. Truthmaker then adds that there must be a state of affairs along the lines of *Fido's being brown*, having its truthmaking constituents essentially. But this addition is not motivated by Truthmaker's primary motivation. For (1)'s truth 'depends on the world' just so long as Fido exists and is brown (see Dodd 2002; McGrath 2003: 682–3). And just so long as one grants that Fido exists and is brown, one does not cheat by saying that (1) is true.

Given only what I have said thus far, it is an open question whether every truth is relevantly like (1). That is, it is an open question whether we can accommodate Truthmaker's primary motivation with respect to every truth without somehow committing ourselves to Truthmaker itself. Chapter 4 explores an alternative to Truthmaker that purports to do just that. As we shall see, our exploration of that alternative will build on points made about Truthmaker below, in this chapter and the next.

II. Necessary Truths

Necessitation (or conditional necessitation) is one ingredient of *making true* (Ch. 1, §§II–III). In fact, for all we have said so far, (conditional) necessitation could be the whole story. That is, it could be that there is nothing more to *making true* than (conditional) necessitation.

For the sake of argument, suppose that there is nothing more. Suppose that for all x and all p, x makes p true if and only if, necessarily, if x exists (and p exists), then p is true. This has the result that each and every existing thing is a truthmaker for every necessary truth. It has this result because, for all x and all p, *necessarily*, p *is true* implies *necessarily, if* x *exists, then* p *is true*.

This result is familiar (see, e.g., Armstrong 2003: 14). David Lewis points it out as soon as he articulates Truthmaker, an articulation that seems to equate *making true* with necessitation:

In a slogan: every truth has a truthmaker. Spelled out at greater length: for any true proposition P, there exists something T such that T's existence strictly implies (necessitates) P. ... if P is a necessary proposition, then for any T whatever, T's existence strictly implies P. So the Truthmaker Principle, as I have stated it, applies only trivially to necessary truths. (2001: 604)

Unlike Lewis, Barry Smith does not say that Truthmaker applies only trivially to necessary truths. Smith says, instead, that Truthmaker does not apply to them at all. For Smith takes Truthmaker to be the view that 'reality constrains the practice of judgment by determining which *contingent* judgments are true' (1999: 274, emphasis added; see also Armstrong 1989b: 88).

So Lewis concedes that Truthmaker applies only trivially to necessary truths.[4] And Smith concedes that it applies not at all. But, I shall argue, neither concession should be acceptable to those who defend Truthmaker in the first place. (I myself am happy to say that at least some necessary truths lack truthmakers, but that is because I think that Truthmaker is false.)

My argument begins by supposing that you deny that there are any mathematical entities. You deny that there are mathematical properties. And you deny that mathematical claims can be, in any sense, reduced to or analysed in terms of or constituted by any of the other objects and properties that you do believe in. Yet you add that Fermat's Last Theorem (FLT) is true.[5]

---

[4] Lewis (2001: 604) goes on to say: 'A non-trivial principle requiring truthmakers for necessary truths would presumably replace strict implication by some more discriminating sort of relevant or paraconsistent implication.' But since the necessitation involved in truthmaking is not a relation between propositions alone (Ch. 1, §III), I do not think it can be captured by any logic of implication. (Lewis here cites Restall (1996); but Restall suggests only a way to keep everything from appropriately necessitating necessary truths of the form $A \vee {\sim}A$; he is silent about other necessary truths.)

[5] FLT says that the following equation has no non-zero integer solutions for $x, y,$ and z where $n > 2$: $x^n + y^n = z^n$.

Truthmaker theorists, let us suppose, think you are cheating. So they charge that, when it comes to the truth of FLT, you do not respect the dependence of what is true on what there is. You plead not guilty. For you say that your left thumb is a (trivial) truthmaker for FLT, since, necessarily, if your left thumb exists, FLT is true.

If your thumb were a truthmaker for FLT, then your affirming your thumb's existence would thereby refute the charge that you cheat. But surely your affirming this does not refute that charge. Instead, your belief in your thumb's existence seems to be totally irrelevant to whether you cheat in endorsing FLT. All of this implies that, even if we call your thumb a 'trivial truthmaker' for FLT, your thumb is not really a truthmaker for FLT. For, again, if it were a truthmaker for FLT, your endorsing its existence would refute the charge that you cheat.

Your thumb is not a truthmaker of any sort for FLT. And, in general, a 'trivial truthmaker' is not really a truthmaker at all. As a result, it is a mistake to say *both* that necessary truths must have truthmakers *and also* that those truthmakers can be trivial. We should not *both* accuse defenders of a necessary truth of cheating unless they offer a truthmaker *and also* acquit them of cheating when they offer a 'trivial truthmaker'. Necessary truths require only 'trivial truthmakers' just in case necessary truths do not require truthmakers at all.

So suppose that necessary truths do not require truthmakers at all. Some might take this to mean that necessary truths are counterexamples to Truthmaker, and therefore that Truthmaker should be rejected outright. But let us not take it that way. Let us take it, instead, as a suggested friendly amendment to Truthmaker. I shall now give four reasons that Truthmaker should not be thus amended, four reasons that those who defend Truthmaker should not ratchet it back so that it applies only to contingent truths.

First, whenever putative cheaters find themselves committed to truthmakerless truths, they can say that those truths are—

just like necessary truths—exempt from the demands of Truthmaker. And it is hard to see how truthmaker theorists can object, in a principled way, to this strategy, once they themselves have exempted some truths from Truthmaker. And so truthmaker theorists, being cheater catchers, should not exempt necessary truths.

Second, recall from Chapter 1 (§I) that Truthmaker is motivated by the idea that 'a truth, any truth, should depend for its truth [on] something "outside" it, in virtue of which it is true' (Armstrong 2004: 7). Obviously enough, this idea about 'a truth, any truth' encompasses necessary truths. So a version of Truthmaker that fails to apply to necessary truths is inconsistent with the intuition that motivated Truthmaker in the first place, the intuition that truth depends substantively on being.

My third reason begins by supposing that *that God exists* is necessarily true. Even though I reject Truthmaker, I think that *that God exists* must have a truthmaker: namely, God. And, more importantly, those who endorse Truthmaker should agree. That is, any truthmaker theorist ought to reject out of hand this conjunction: *that God exists* is necessarily true and *that God exists* has no truthmaker. Therefore, it is false that Truthmaker should make no demands on necessary truths. Even a ratcheted-back version of Truthmaker must recognize that some purported necessary truths would require truthmakers.

Suppose our ratcheted-back version of Truthmaker does recognize this. Nevertheless, it still says that some necessary truths do not need truthmakers. Which necessary truths do not? It seems to be all and only those necessary truths for which we can find no truthmaker. For example, it is hard to come up with an intuitively satisfying truthmaker for FLT. So we exempt FLT from the demands of Truthmaker. On the other hand, if we did locate a truthmaker for FLT, I bet that we would insist that FLT requires a truthmaker.

This way of proceeding robs Truthmaker of any pretensions to be a principled catcher of cheaters that may have survived Truthmaker's descent from being entirely unrestricted to exempting all necessary truths. For truthmaker theorists who thus proceed surely have no principled way to object to wily cheaters who proceed likewise. These are the cheaters who, when faced with some apparently truthmakerless truths, simply amend Truthmaker—perhaps even one truth at a time—so that those truths are not within its purview.

The fourth and final reason that Truthmaker should not exempt necessary truths will appeal only to those who accept the correspondence theory of truth and see it as motivating Truthmaker. But this includes many of the most prominent truthmaker theorists (Ch. 1, §I). Suppose, for the sake of argument, that the correspondence theory is correct. Then it is analytic that each necessary truth, in virtue of being true, corresponds to something. For thus corresponding is *what it is* to be true. Lest the correspondence theory fail to motivate Truthmaker, that to which a truth corresponds is thereby a truthmaker for that truth. So necessary truths have truthmakers.

In light of the above four reasons, truthmaker theorists should insist that necessary truths have genuine (non-trivial) truthmakers. Not everything is a genuine truthmaker for each necessary truth. But everything necessitates each necessary truth. Therefore, there is more to *making true* than mere necessitation.

One way of putting the principal motivation for Truthmaker suggests what this 'more' might be. Recall Lewis's remark that Truthmaker aims to preserve something 'right and important and underappreciated. What's right, roughly speaking, is that truths must have *things* as their subject matter' (Lewis 1999*a*: 206). Suppose that truths are about things. And suppose that Truthmaker does aim to preserve this. Then Truthmaker should say that each truth's truthmaker is that which that truth is about. For only then would the existence of a truthmaker for a truth imply that there is something that that truth is about.

If all this is right, then truths are about things, which things are the truthmakers for those truths. Above I noted that your thumb fails to be a genuine truthmaker for FLT. But I did not explain why it fails. I can now explain. Even though your thumb's existence necessitates FLT's truth, FLT is not about your thumb. And *bona fide* truthmakers are that which their respective truths are about.

George Molnar tells us: 'There are philosophers who hold that whereas contingent truths need a truthmaker, necessary truths do not.'[6]

Molnar opposes these philosophers, at least when it comes to 'material' necessary truths.

Although there may be some necessary truths that are not in need of truthmakers, namely, formal truths (the truth-functional tautologies), material necessary statements are, *prima facie*, just modally strong claims about the world .... Materially necessary truths are claims about the world that are true not just 'as things are' but 'as things are and no matter how things could be'. It is *qua* claim about the world that true statements need a truthmaker and not *qua* modally weak claim. The thesis that necessary truths do not make any claims about the world has never struck me as having any plausibility except when applied to tautologies. (Molnar 2000: 74–5)

Molnar suggests that 'material truths' are about the world, but 'formal truths' are not. So he would resist Lewis's claim that all truths are about things. Rather, Molnar would say that only material truths are about things. And so he requires truthmakers for material necessary truths but not for formal necessary truths.

---

[6] Armstrong, Molnar, and others give the impression that an army of philosophers runs about (presumably, runs about Australia) insisting on genuine truthmakers for all and only contingent truths. But these philosophers are not cited, and few (if any) philosophers unequivocally endorse this position in print. (Above I quoted Smith as saying that only contingent truths have truthmakers, but in the same article he denies that all contingent truths have truthmakers (see Smith 1999: 284–5).)

I think that *that bachelors are bachelors* is about things: namely, bachelors (see Sider 2003: 200). This is one reason that I do not go along with all that Molnar says above. Moreover, I think that the primary bearers of truth are propositions, rather than (for example) sentence tokens; and I have doubts about the material/formal distinction as applied to propositions, as opposed to (for example) sentence tokens. This is a second reason that I am not inclined to go along with Molnar here.

But set those reasons aside. For even if Molnar is right, some necessary truths have genuine truthmakers. So we can conclude that necessitation is not all there is to *making true*. Moreover, the idea that a truth is somehow about its truthmaker is implicit in how Molnar draws the material/formal distinction. Thus Molnar's overall position here supports, rather than undermines, the two main conclusions of this section.

III. More on a Truth's Being about its Truthmaker

The two main conclusions of the previous section were that (conditional) necessitation is not the whole of *making true* and that a truthmaker must be that which its truth is about. This section presents four more arguments for those same two conclusions. But this section's arguments, unlike those of the previous section, have nothing to do with necessary truths. So even those truthmaker theorists who misguidedly exempt necessary truths from Truthmaker's demands should still endorse the two main conclusions of the previous section.

Barry Smith denies that necessitation is the *making true* relation. But his denial has nothing to do with necessary truths. Smith says: 'There are malignant necessitators. Suppose God wills that John kiss Mary now. God's willing act thereby necessitates the truth of "John is kissing Mary". (For Malebranche, all necessitation is of this sort.) But God's act is not a truth-maker for this judgment' (Smith 1999: 278). Suppose God's willing really does necessitate *that John is kissing Mary*. Nevertheless, that willing is not a truthmaker for *that John is kissing Mary*. Therefore it is false that *making true* is nothing more than necessitation.

That John is kissing Mary is about John's kissing, but not about God's willing. This is the reason, I say, that God's willing does not make *that John is kissing Mary* true. Smith draws the same conclusion, saying that 'A truthmaker for a given judgment must be [that] which the judgment is *about*, must satisfy some relevance constraint' (1999: 279).

We could come up with many relevantly similar examples involving God's willing (or believing). These examples give us this section's first reason for concluding that the relation of *making true* is more than mere necessitation. And generalizing from these examples gives us its first reason for concluding that a truth must be about its truthmaker.

A 'world-bound' individual exists in only one possible world. An actual world-bound individual exists in only the actual world. So an actual world-bound individual exists in only those worlds (i.e., the actual world) in which every (actual) truth is true. Thus any such individual necessitates every truth. If *making true* were just necessitation, then every (actual) world-bound individual would be a truthmaker for every truth. But, as Lewis (2001: 604) rightly says of this result: 'That will never do—truthmaking was not meant to be so easy.' This implies that *making true* is not just necessitation.

And suppose there actually is a world-bound individual. Suppose it is a certain electron. *That a human exists* is necessitated by that electron. But it is not in any way about that electron, which explains why that electron is not its truthmaker. On the other hand, *that a world-bound individual exists* is not only necessitated by, but is also about, that electron. This explains why that electron is a truthmaker for *that a world-bound individual exists*. Generalizing from this case, we get our second reason for concluding not only that *making true* is more than necessitation, but also that truths are about their truthmakers.

Truthmaker theorists often say that a truthmaker *explains* that which it makes true:

Truthmaker theory is a theory of the groundedness of truth-values. Minimally, such a theory should enable one to identify whatever it is that explains why the truth-bearers have the truth-values they have. (Molnar 2000: 82)

[Truthmakers] are entities whose entire *raison d'être* is to explain what makes a linguistic item true. (Bigelow 1988: 121)

That a human exists is true because I (among others) exist. And so, in some sense of 'explain', I myself explain the truth of *that a human exists*. Contrast this with the state of affairs of *Fido's having the property of being such that a human exists*. *That a human exists* is not true because that state of affairs involving Fido exists. So that state does not explain the truth of *that a human exists*. Assuming truthmaking involves explanation, that state is not a truthmaker for *that a human exists*. But that state necessitates *that a human exists*. So necessitation is not sufficient for *making true*.

Moreover, that truthmaking involves explanation suggests that a truth must be about its truthmaker. For my explaining the truth of *that a human exists* seems to imply that that truth is about me. And it seems that the state of *Fido's being such that a human exists* fails to explain the truth of *that a human exists* because that truth is not about that state. In fact, I suspect that the idea that a truth must be explained by its truthmaker just is the idea that a truth must be appropriately about its truthmaker. And so we have our third reason.

Suppose that if a proposition is true, that proposition has the property of *being true*. Add to this Truthmaker's commitment to states of affairs (§I). Then we can conclude that, for any proposition *p*, if *p* is true, then there is the state of affairs of p's

being true. Necessarily, if the state of p*'s being true* exists, then
p is true.[7] This shows that necessitation is not sufficient for
truthmaking. For it is false that, for all *p*, the state of p*'s being
true* is a truthmaker for *p*.

It had better be false. Recall:

(2) If Queen Elizabeth II had been born in seventeenth-
century Japan, she would have been a samurai warrior.

(2)'s truthmaker, some might say, is the state of affairs of
(2)'s being true. Assuming that there are such states of affairs,
a 'truthmaker' along these lines exists for any true claim
whatsoever. If such 'truthmakers' were acceptable, then the
objection that a claim lacks a truthmaker would presuppose
that that claim was not true. But, presumably, it is possible for
Truthmaker to catch cheaters without begging the question
in this way. So it is false that for all *p*, the state of p*'s being
true* is a truthmaker for *p*. This is a fourth reason to say that
necessitation is not the whole of *making true*.

This fourth reason to say that necessitation is not the whole
of *making true* points toward our fourth reason to say that truths
are about their truthmakers. Consider that for some (though
not for every) proposition *p*, p*'s being true* is a truthmaker for
p. For example:

(3) There is at least one true proposition.

For each true proposition, that proposition's being true is a
truthmaker for (3). (Compare: each brown dog's being brown
is a truthmaker for *that there is at least one brown dog*.) So *(3)'s
being true* is a truthmaker for (3).

---

[7] This assumes that if this state exists, it has *p* and *being true* as essential
constituents. The above example involving the state of affairs of *Fido's having the
property of being such that a human exists* makes a similar assumption. Truthmaker
theorists should grant these assumptions, given Truthmaker's commitments
regarding the essential constituents of states of affairs (§I).

(3)'s being true is a truthmaker for (3). But surely *(2)'s being true* is not a truthmaker for (2), the claim about Her Royal Highness's counterfactual career. This difference between (2) and (3) can be explained as follows. (3) is about each proposition's being true and, therefore, is about *(3)'s being true*. (2) is not about *(2)'s being true*. This explanation of this difference between (2) and (3) supports the idea that a truth must be about its truthmaker.

Truthmaker says that, for each truth, there exists something that is its truthmaker. The last two sections have shown that a truth must be *about* its truthmaker. So Truthmaker implies that, for each truth, there exists something that that truth is about. This implication is more substantive than it might appear. For it might appear to follow from the following two claims. First, grasping or understanding a proposition involves knowing what that proposition is about; and so, obviously, every proposition (and so every truth) that can be grasped is about something; and so, let us grant, every proposition (and so every truth) is about something.[8] Second, if a truth is about something, then there exists something that that truth is about. From these two claims it follows, so it might appear, that for any truth, there exists something that that truth is about.

But this reasoning is flawed. Consider a ghost story. That story, naturally enough, is about ghosts. If I did not know that it was about ghosts, I would not understand that story. But none of this implies that there are some things—namely, ghosts—that are such that that story is about them. Instead, that story's being 'about ghosts' implies only something regarding the nature of the story.

Similarly, the obvious way in which every proposition (and so every truth) is 'about something' is not a matter of *there being*

---

[8] Perhaps all propositions can be grasped. Or perhaps all graspable propositions' being 'about something' is inductive evidence that all propositions, even the ungraspable ones, are about something.

something that that proposition is about. After all, to know what a proposition is 'about' in this sense is not to know of some object or state of affairs to which that proposition is related by an *aboutness* relation. Rather, it is to understand or grasp that proposition.

So we should not conflate Truthmaker's claim that, for every truth, there exists something or other that that truth is about with the fairly obvious and innocuous claim that every truth is 'about something'. Unlike this fairly obvious and innocuous claim, Truthmaker is asserting that there is an *aboutness* relation and that, for each true *p*, there is some *x* such that *p* is thus related to *x*.

One might understand a proposition perfectly and still not know what it is about, in the sense of 'about' that is central to Truthmaker. For example, one could understand *that a human exists* perfectly without knowing that you or I exist, even though, in Truthmaker's sense of 'about', *that a human exists* is about each of its truthmakers, and so is about you and is also about me.

Our insight into Truthmaker's *aboutness* relation comes from examples. For instance, as just noted, *that a human exists* is, in Truthmaker's sense of 'about', about you and about me. Likewise, *that Fido is brown* is thus about the state of affairs of *Fido's being brown*. And *that John is kissing Mary* is thus about *John's kissing Mary*. Contrast these examples with the following. *That a human exists* is not thus about a world-bound individual (unless that world-bound individual happens to be human). FLT fails to be thus about your left thumb. And for many propositions *p*, the state of *p's being true* is not what *p* is about. Many other examples of entities that both necessitate a truth and are, moreover, what that truth is about can be found in this and the previous section. The same goes for examples of entities that necessitate a truth but are not what that truth is about.

I think that these examples give us an adequate grasp of the relevant *aboutness* relation. But I offer no analysis of that relation. Nor do I have an absolutely decisive rebuttal for the sceptic who objects that, the above examples notwithstanding, we cannot really make sense of Truthmaker's *aboutness* relation. On the contrary, I have a bit of sympathy for this objection. But no truthmaker theorist should. For to deny that we can make sense of the relevant *aboutness* relation is to deny that we can make sense of Truthmaker. This is because, as the above two sections should have made clear, Truthmaker requires a truth to be appropriately about its truthmaker.

In what follows, I shall give Truthmaker the benefit of the doubt. That is, I shall assume that we can make sense of Truthmaker's *aboutness* relation. Moreover, in what follows, I shall upon occasion disqualify a wannabe truthmaker on the grounds that it fails to be what the relevant truth is thus about, even though it necessitates that truth. One might wonder whether I am right that the aspiring truthmaker is not—in the relevant sense of 'about'—about that truth. To decide, we must consider whether the potential truthmaker is relevantly like the examples of necessitating entities that fail to be truthmakers discussed in this and the preceding section. These examples are our guide.

We should conclude that *making true* involves *aboutness*. But we should also stand by the previous chapter's point that *making true* implies (conditional) necessitation. For even if there were nothing more to *making true* than a proposition's being related to that which makes it true by *aboutness*, *making true* would still imply necessitation. This is because that to which a proposition stands in the *aboutness* relation thereby necessitates that proposition. At least, I lose my (admittedly somewhat shaky) grip on *aboutness* if I add that that which a truth is relevantly about need not (even conditionally) necessitate that truth. So I shall assume that Truthmaker implies not only that truths are about their respective truth-makers but also that truthmakers necessitate their respective truths.

IV. Suspicious Properties

Truthmaker theorists think that if an object has a property, there is the state of affairs of that object's having that property (§I). So they think that, just so long as Elizabeth II Regina has the relevant property, there is the state of affairs of *Elizabeth II's having the property of being such that, had she been born 400 years ago in Japan, she would have been a samurai warrior*.

This state—if there is such a state—is arguably a truthmaker for

(2) If Queen Elizabeth II had been born in seventeenth-century Japan, she would have been a samurai warrior.

For (2) is not only necessitated by this state, but is also plausibly appropriately *about* this state. Again, it is plausible that (2) is appropriately about Elizabeth's being such that, had she been born 400 years ago in Japan, she would have been a samurai warrior. At the very least, this state has a better shot at making (2) true than your thumb has at making FLT true.

No one has explicitly endorsed reconciling (2) with Truth-maker via the above strategy. But that strategy has not lain idle. For consider not (2), but rather:

(4) If Curley had been offered a $35,000 bribe, he would have freely taken it.

Proponents of claims like (4) have often been accused of cheating. Francisco Suarez provides a defence against that accusation. A Suarezian defence of (4) turns on the idea that Curley has the property of *being such that had he been offered a $35,000 bribe, he would have freely taken it* (see Adams 1987: 81–82).

Or consider presentism. Presentism allows that there are truths about the past (e.g., *that the Trojans were conquered*). But it denies that there are merely past states (e.g., *the state of the Trojans being conquered*) to make them true. So presentism is commonly charged with cheating.

Following Lucretius (1994: 21), John Bigelow says: 'One of the things that exists is the whole world, the totality of things that exist. The world can have properties and accidents, just as its parts may have. It is a present property of the world, that it is a world in which Helen was abducted and the Trojans were conquered' (1996: 46). 'Lucretianism' suggests presentist-friendly truthmakers for claims about the past. For example, it suggests that the state of affairs of *the universe's being such that the Trojans were conquered* is a truthmaker for *that the Trojans were conquered*.

Lucretian and Suarezian properties receive further attention in Chapters 6 and 7, respectively. I bring these properties up now just to show that Truthmaker will be unable to catch certain cheaters unless it keeps these properties from playing a role in truthmaking. Catching cheaters is a principal motivation for Truthmaker. Moreover, Truthmaker is of interest in this book largely because it threatens to rule out this or that philosophical theory. So let us better equip Truthmaker to catch cheaters.

Let Truthmaker say that truthmakers cannot be constituted by 'suspicious properties'. Moreover, let a fully articulated Truthmaker tell us which properties really are suspicious. Now we can resist suspect attempts to accommodate Truthmaker. For example, we can block the above defence of (2) by deeming to be suspicious the property of *being such that, had she been born 400 years ago in Japan, she would have been a samurai warrior*.[9]

Suppose that *being such that, had she been born 400 years ago in Japan, she would have been a samurai warrior* really is suspicious. Nevertheless, no analysis of *being true* will tell us that it is suspicious. More generally, no analysis of *being true* says which properties are suspicious. But a fully articulated Truthmaker

---

[9] In Ch. 1 (§I), we saw that since Truthmaker articulates a non-trivial way for all truths to depend on being, Truthmaker can catch some cheaters. But to equip Truthmaker to catch all cheaters, we now see, we must take it to judge some properties to be suspicious.

tells us which properties are suspicious. And so no analysis of *being true* entails Truthmaker. So the correspondence theory of truth, which purports to analyse *being true*, fails to entail Truthmaker. (This is one more reason, in addition to those presented in the previous chapter, to deny that the correspondence theory of truth is identical with Truthmaker.)

To catch certain cheaters, Truthmaker must deem some properties to be suspicious. So a fully articulated Truthmaker would tell us which properties are suspicious and which are not. For example, a fully articulated Truthmaker might say that the only non-suspicious properties are qualitative categorical properties exemplified by points of spacetime. This version of Truthmaker says that each truth is made true by a state (or states) of such properties' being exemplified. Indeed, since truths are appropriately about their truthmakers, this version of Truthmaker says that each and every truth is thus about a distribution of point-sized quality instances.

This version of Truthmaker takes a stand on which properties are suspicious. But it does so by legislating that all truths are—in Truthmaker's sense of 'about'—about qualitative categorical properties exemplified by points of spacetime. As a result, this version of Truthmaker endorses a controversial and stridently reductive metaphysics. Naturally enough, some philosophical theories are inconsistent with this metaphysics, but this hardly makes them cheaters!

Of course, defenders of Truthmaker can exchange this metaphysics for one that is less austere. But the point remains the same. A fully articulated Truthmaker contains a full account of which properties are suspicious. A full account of which properties are suspicious is itself a full-blown metaphysics. Thus a fully articulated Truthmaker is not a neutral litmus test that competing theories must pass to be taken seriously. Instead, it is one of the competitors.

Perhaps it is better to operate with only a partially articulated version of Truthmaker, one that identifies only some suspicious properties, rather than all. Some partially articulated versions of Truthmaker are both fairly metaphysically ecumenical and also able to catch some cheaters. For example, philosophers of varying metaphysical inclinations will accept that *being such that, had she been born 400 years ago in Japan, she would have been a samurai warrior* is suspicious. And this is probably all that is required to mount a Truthmaker-based attack on (2).

But familiar Truthmaker-based attacks on other alleged cheaters require more. For example, Truthmaker's standard objection to presentism is that, given presentism, there is nothing that necessitates true claims about the past. The whole point of the Lucretian properties discussed above is to block just this objection. So the standard Truthmaker-based attack on presentism succeeds only if it deems Lucretian properties to be suspicious.

More generally, Truthmaker-based attacks on supposed cheaters often require Truthmaker to deem to be suspicious a property that the alleged cheaters themselves might well claim is acceptable. In such cases, Truthmaker-based controversy over this or that theory turns out to be controversy over this or that property. And as this or that property is judged to be suspicious—and so as this or that theory is rejected—Truthmaker itself is thereby more fully articulated. In this way, any well-articulated version of Truthmaker presupposes that certain theories should be rejected. So any well-articulated version of Truthmaker fails to be an independent reason to reject some (but not all) of the theories that violate it.

3

NEGATIVE EXISTENTIALS

TRUTHMAKER says that each truth has a truthmaker. So Truth-maker implies that, for each truth, there is some entity or other whose mere existence necessitates that truth. Moreover, Truthmaker implies that each truth is in some way about the positively existing entity that is its truthmaker. And, finally, Truthmaker implies that a truthmaker cannot be constituted by suspicious properties. This chapter argues that these implications cause trouble for Truthmaker when it comes to negative existentials and universal generalizations.

I. Negative Existentials Need Truthmakers

This chapter focuses mainly on negative existentials, which assert that something fails to exist. For example:

(1) Hobbits do not exist.

We shall also consider universal generalizations, such as:

(2) All ravens are black.

(2) might seem to be easily handled by Truthmaker: (2) is jointly made true by the state of affairs of this raven's being black, and that raven's being black and so on, for each and every raven. Similarly, one might suggest that (2) is made true by the 'sum' of these states of affairs. But none of this will do.

For it is possible for all those states of affairs to exist and (2) to be false, since it is possible that all our black ravens exist and a white one besides.[1]

Spooked by (1) and (2), timid truthmaker theorists might say that such truths do not need truthmakers (see, e.g., Mulligan, Simons, and Smith 1984: 315 and Smith 1999: 285). Their idea is not that negative existentials are counterexamples to Truthmaker, and therefore that Truthmaker is false. They aim, instead, to propose a friendly amendment to Truthmaker. But there are four reasons that Truthmaker's advocates should not amend it to exempt negative existentials (or universal generalizations).[2]

First, suppose we came up with plausible truthmakers for each and every true negative existential. Then, I think, truthmaker theorists would embrace full-blown Truthmaker, which demands truthmakers for all truths, including true negative existentials. This suggests that the only reason to scale back Truthmaker to exempt negative existentials is that there do not seem to be truthmakers for negative existentials.

Truthmaker theorists who proceed in this way have no principled objection to the cheater who, when confronted with her own apparently truthmakerless truths, scales back Truthmaker accordingly. For this cheater is simply adopting the strategy of the timid truthmaker theorist, concluding that since there do not seem to be any truthmakers for a certain kind of truth, none are required.

Second, Truthmaker is driven by the intuition or insight or conviction or idea that 'a truth, any truth' depends on being. This intuition does not exempt negative existentials. One might reply that negative existential truths are about *what*

---

[1] Negative existentials and universal generalizations are not the only truths that create particular difficulties for Truthmaker. Also problematic are truths that deny an object is a certain way (see Russell 1985: 74; 1919: 1–6).

[2] The first three of these reasons are variations on three reasons that Truthmaker should not be curtailed to exempt necessary truths (Ch. 2, §II).

does not exist. Therefore, so this reply goes, it is intuitive that they—and they alone—do not depend for their truth on *what exists.* But I deny that if we set aside the intuition that 'a truth, any truth' depends on being, we are left with the equally compelling intuition that all truths *except negative existentials* depend on being.

That is, I deny that we have the gerrymandered intuition that truths about *what exists* and *what was* and *what will be* and *what should be* and *what could be* and *what would be* and *what might be* and *what must be* and even *how existing things are not* all depend on being—but truths about what *does not exist* do not so depend. So Truthmaker amended to exempt only negative existentials not only runs counter to the intuition that is Truthmaker's primary motivation, but also fails to be motivated by any other compelling intuition about truth's dependence on being.

Third, suppose that truth is correspondence. Then it is analytic that each negative existential truth, in virtue of being true, corresponds to something. And so, unless they can explain why that to which a negative existential corresponds fails to make that negative existential true, truthmaker theorists should say that true negative existentials have truthmakers. Obviously, this third reason has no purchase on truthmaker theorists who reject the correspondence theory of truth.

Fourth, suppose that there is a sorcerer bent on keeping glass G from shattering. Suppose that if G were struck, the sorcerer would change G's microstructure so that it would not shatter (the example is from Lewis 1999*b*: 138). Then the following dispositional conditional is false:

(3) If glass G were struck, then G would shatter.

Conversely, if (3) is true, then there is no such sorcerer. That is, (3) entails that there is no sorcerer who, were G to be struck, would change G's microstructure so that it would not shatter.

If (3) has a truthmaker, then that truthmaker, by its mere existence, necessitates the truth of (3). That truthmaker thereby necessitates the truth of every claim that (3) entails. And so if (3) has a truthmaker, there is something that, by its mere existence, necessitates the truth of *that there is no sorcerer who would keep G from shattering, were G to be struck.* Conversely, if nothing at all thus necessitates negative existentials, then (3) has no truthmaker, and, more generally, neither do any other dispositional conditionals. (More on dispositional conditionals in Ch. 7, §III.)

All self-described truthmaker theorists insist that dispositional conditionals have truthmakers. Therefore, they should all insist that, with respect to each negative existential entailed by a true dispositional conditional, there is something that, by its mere existence, necessitates the truth of that negative existential. Moreover, they should insist that that something, since it is the truthmaker for a dispositional conditional, is not constituted by suspicious properties. Nor is that something—again, since it is a truthmaker for a dispositional conditional—going to be anything along the lines of *(3)'s being true* or *God's believing that there is no sorcerer who would keep G from shattering, were G to be struck.*

Defenders of Truthmaker are motivated to deny that negative existentials have truthmakers only because it seems that nothing, by its mere existence, necessitates a negative existential. More carefully, they are motivated to deny this only because it seems that the only things that, by their mere existence, could necessitate negative existentials would be states constituted by suspicious properties or states relevantly like *God's believing* p or p's *being true*. But this motivation has been completely undercut. A commitment to truthmakers for dispositional conditionals brings with it a commitment to the claim that, at least for each negative existential entailed by a true dispositional conditional, there exists something that necessitates that negative existential, something neither constituted by suspicious properties nor remotely like *God's believing* p or p's *being true*. So truthmaker theorists should say that all such negative existentials have truthmakers. I think it would then be both unprincipled and unmotivated to persist in saying that other true negative existentials lack truthmakers. This concludes the fourth reason that truthmaker theorists should say that true negative existentials have truthmakers.

Truthmaker theorists should say that negative existential truths have truthmakers. Moreover, they should say something about what those truthmakers are like. For there are many true negative existentials, none of which seems at first glance to have a truthmaker. And truthmaker theorists who say absolutely nothing about what the truthmakers for negative existentials are like have no principled objection to the cheater who follows suit. This is the cheater who says: 'I cannot tell you what the truthmakers for claims about the past [or counterfactuals or ...] are like—and I know that given my ontology it looks for all the world like they lack truthmakers—but I do not cheat because I still say that each has a truthmaker.'

II. Two Inadequate Accounts that No One Defends

David Armstrong says more about the truthmakers for negative existentials than does any other truthmaker theorist. And we shall consider Armstrong's account of those truthmakers. But first I want to consider two accounts that are, to the best of my knowledge, defended nowhere in print. They are still worth a look. For the first might seem to be a natural corollary of a Fregean approach to existence claims. And the issues raised in examining the second will prove useful when we turn to Armstrong's account.

A Fregean about existence claims would say that *that hobbits do not exist* is nothing other than the claim that *being a hobbit* is not exemplified (Frege 1997*b*; Toner 2006). And so, one might think, a Fregean should say that *that hobbits do not exist* is made true by *being a hobbit*'s failing to be exemplified—and likewise, *mutatis mutandis*, for every other negative existential.

A property's failing to be exemplified just is its having no instances. Therefore, *being a hobbit*'s failing to be exemplified amounts to the following: there is that property, and there are no hobbits. But none of this suggests a truthmaker for *that hobbits do not exist*. For none of this suggests anything that, by its mere existence, necessitates the truth of *that hobbits do not exist*.[3] More generally, Fregeanism about existence claims does not deliver truthmakers for negative existentials.

Nevertheless, one might claim that whenever *being a hobbit* does fail to be exemplified, there is always a state of affairs of *being a hobbit*'s exemplifying the property of *failing to be exemplified*. That state, by its mere existence, would necessitate the truth of *that hobbits do not exist*. So one might claim that this state is the truthmaker for *that hobbits do not exist*. But I have three objections to the idea that this state is the truthmaker for that truth and, more generally, to the idea that a negative existential is made true by the relevant property's exemplifying *failing to be exemplified*.

My first objection begins by pointing out that the property of *failing to be exemplified* is not a relation in which *being a hobbit* stands to something. So it is a monadic property. Moreover, it is not a monadic property that is exemplified because of some relation in which its bearer stands to something else.[4] In this way, *failing to be exemplified* is not merely monadic; it is

---

[3] *Being a hobbit* cannot itself be the truthmaker, since—assuming that *that hobbits do not exist* is only contingently true—that property fails to necessitate that claim. But perhaps *that hobbits do not exist* is necessarily true (see Kripke 1980: 156–8). If so, replace (1) with *that white ravens do not exist*. And adapt my remarks to follow to the proposal that *that white ravens do not exist* is made true by the state of *being a white raven*'s failing to be exemplified.

[4] Some monadic properties (such as *being married*) are exemplified because of how their bearer is related to something else (such as standing in the *being married to* relation to something else). But *failing to be exemplified* is not like this. For the solution now being considered does not say that, e.g., *being a hobbit* exemplifies

thoroughly non-relational. Nevertheless, *failing to be exemplified* is not intrinsic. For example, it can be lost simply in virtue of a change in its bearer's environment.

(Thus we have an important way in which this account of the truthmaker for *that hobbits do not exist* resembles the other accounts discussed below, accounts which otherwise seem quite different from it. For, as we shall see, all these accounts rely on some sort of thoroughly non-relational but nevertheless non-intrinsic property. The property we shall focus on in much of this chapter is *being such that there is nothing more in the universe*.)

As already noted, the Fregean view of existence claims—in particular, the Fregean view that *that hobbits do not exist* asserts that the property of *being a hobbit* is not exemplified—delivers no account of the truthmaker for *that hobbits do not exist*. So it fails to deliver the account we are now considering. In particular, it does not imply that there is a non-intrinsic but non-relational property of *failing to be exemplified*, which cannot possibly be exemplified by a property if instances of that property exist. And, to use the terminology of Chapter 2 (§IV), I object that *failing to be exemplified* is suspicious. Similarly, I object that the state of affairs of *being a hobbit*'s having that property is an implausible *ad hoc* device whose sole purpose is to placate Truthmaker.

Second, suppose, for the sake of argument, that we allow the exemplification of *failing to be exemplified* by various properties to placate Truthmaker with respect to negative existentials. If Truthmaker can thus be placated, then it can be placated by other *ad hoc* devices. For example, presentists could claim that *that the Trojans were conquered* is made true by the state of affairs of the property of *being conquered* and the property of *being Trojans* being related by *having been co-exemplified*.

---

failing to be exemplified because there exists some x such that *being a hobbit* is appropriately related to x.

This way of accommodating Truthmaker seems to be no more objectionable than accommodating Truthmaker by way of *failing to be exemplified*. This illustrates that the account of truthmakers for negative existentials here being considered undermines Truthmaker's ability to catch cheaters.

Third, recall that truths must be, in an appropriate sense of 'about', about their truthmakers (Ch. 2, §§II–III). This is why, for example, *that the Trojans were conquered* cannot be made true by the state of affairs of *that the Trojans were conquered's being true*, even though that state necessitates that claim. For *that the Trojans were conquered* is not appropriately about that state. Similarly, I say that *that the Trojans were conquered* is not appropriately about two abstract properties and a relation between them. So the presentist strategy for accommodating Truthmaker just considered fails. But so too does the parallel strategy involving negative existentials. For it is simply false that *that hobbits do not exist* is appropriately about a property's *having a non-relational property*.

I want to emphasize that this is simply false even if the Fregean account of claims about existence is correct. For even if *that hobbits do not exist* really is about the property of *being a hobbit's* not being exemplified, it is not about that property's having a non-relational property. So it is not made true by the state of *being a hobbit's* having a non-relational property. Thus it is not made true by the state of *being a hobbit's* having the property of *failing to be exemplified*. The only plausible way I see to resist this third objection is to abandon the requirement that a truth must stand in the *aboutness* relation to its truthmaker, but that would be to abandon Truthmaker itself (Ch. 2, §III).

Let us turn to a second account of the truthmakers for negative existentials. This account says that there is a property of *being such that there are no hobbits*. This is a property that, of necessity, is exemplified if and only if hobbits do not exist. And, according to this account, *that hobbits do not exist* is made true by the state of affairs of *the universe's having the property of being such that there are no hobbits.*[5] More generally, this account says that each negative existential is made true by the state of affairs of the universe's having the property of being such that there are none of the relevant entities. I have three objections to this account.[6]

My first objection begins by asking us to consider not the universe's properties, but rather my properties. In particular, suppose that I have the property of *being such that there are no hobbits.* The state of affairs of my having that property necessitates *that hobbits do not exist.* But that state is not a truthmaker for that claim. It is not that claim's truthmaker, because truths are about their truthmakers. And *that hobbits do not exist* is not about my having any property. So it is not about my having the property of *being such that there are no hobbits.*

That hobbits do not exist is not about my having a property. Nor is it about your having a property. Nor is it about anything else having a property—not even the universe. Truths are about their truthmakers. So I conclude that *that hobbits do not exist* is not made true by the universe's having the property of *being such that there are no hobbits.*

Some might reply that the state of my having the property of *being such that there are no hobbits* is a philosopher's invention.

---

[5] Suppose there is no universe. That is, suppose that no entity exists which has as proper parts all other existing entities. Then, instead of saying that the universe exemplifies *being such that there are no hobbits*, we could say that all existing entities are related by the *no hobbiting* relation. Necessarily, this relation holds between every existing thing if and only if there are no hobbits. The points below concerning properties like *being such that there are no hobbits* can easily be adapted to relations like *no hobbiting.*

[6] Bertrand Russell would say that the truthmaker for *that hobbits do not exist* is the general fact of everything's being a non-hobbit. (This is a general negative fact, since it has to do with how everything is not.) Similarly, he would have another general fact, the fact of everything's failing to be a non-black raven, making true *that all ravens are black.* It is unclear how close Russell's approach is to the account now being discussed in the text—that depends on the nature of his sundry general facts. But about general facts he says only: 'I do not profess to know what the right analysis of general facts is. It is an exceedingly difficult question, and one which I should very much like to see studied' (1985: 103).

On the other hand, their reply continues, the universe's *being such that there are no hobbits* is no such invention; it is, instead, nothing more than there being no hobbits (in the universe); and surely it is right that *that hobbits do not exist* is about there being no hobbits.

I agree that *that hobbits do not exist* is 'about there being no hobbits'. But this does not suggest a truthmaker for *that hobbits do not exist*; nor is it the proposal to which I am objecting. That proposal says that there is a large object—an object composed of every existing entity, the object to which 'the universe' refers—that exemplifies a certain property, the property of *being such that there are no hobbits*. The state of that large object's having that special property is no less of a philosopher's invention than is the state of my having that same special property. (Indeed, it may be more of a philosopher's invention, since the large object referred to by 'the universe' is arguably itself a philosopher's invention, but I myself most definitely am not.) Moreover, I add that neither state is fitter than the other to be that which *that hobbits do not exist* is about; so neither is fitter than the other to be the truthmaker for that claim.

There is a second objection to the proposal that *that hobbits do not exist* is made true by the universe's having the property of *being such that there are no hobbits*. That proposal threatens to gut Truthmaker of its ability to catch cheaters. For consider once again:

(4) If Queen Elizabeth II had been born in seventeenth-century Japan, she would have been a samurai warrior.

Suppose we object that (4) cannot be true because it has no truthmaker. Defenders of (4) can reply that it is made true by the universe's exemplifying the property of *being such that were Elizabeth II to have been born in seventeenth-century Japan, she would have been a samurai warrior*. Or perhaps they will reply that (4)'s truthmaker is the state of affairs of Elizabeth herself, rather than the entire universe, exemplifying that property.

This feels like a cheat. For *being such that were Elizabeth II to have been born in seventeenth-century Japan, she would have been a samurai warrior* seems to be suspicious. But as far as legitimately constituting a truthmaker goes, that property is not obviously worse than *being such that there are no hobbits*. Indeed, as far as being suspicious goes, I think the properties stand or fall together.

The third objection takes some time to defend. The objection is that this account of truthmakers for negative existentials is self-undermining. This is because reflection on the properties that it invokes leads naturally to abandoning it for a different account.

We have been considering an account that says that the state of affairs of *the universe's having the property of being such that there are no hobbits* is the truthmaker for (1): Hobbits do not exist. Similarly, this account says that *the universe's having the property of being such that there are no non-black ravens* is the truthmaker for (2): All ravens are black. And so on for every negative existential truth and general truth.

This account implies that the universe has properties like *being such that there are no hobbits*, *being such that there are no non-black ravens*, and so on. Those who defend this account should insist that these special properties are not primitive. That is, they should say that these properties are built up out of, or analysable in terms of, or reducible to, other properties. For no one should want to posit a different *primitive* property for every negative existential truth and for every general truth.

Moreover, the charge that *being such that there are no hobbits* is suspicious, and so that relying on it in truthmaking is cheating, seems irresistible if this property is alleged to be primitive. To see why I say this, imagine that someone relies on this property in truthmaking: *being such that were Elizabeth II to have been born in seventeenth-century Japan, she would have been a samurai warrior*. This seems like a cheat. And the cheating seems even more flagrant if he goes on to add that that property is primitive. Relatedly, truthmaker theorists who themselves rely on primitive properties like *being such that there are no hobbits* forfeit any principled objection to cheaters who not only rely on their own made-to-order properties, but who also add that those properties are primitive.

So let us assume that properties like *being such that there are no hobbits* are not supposed to be primitive. Rather, they are supposed to be analysed in terms of, or reduced to, other properties (and relations). Suppose that *being a bachelor* is analysed as (or reduced to) *being unmarried*, *being eligible*, and *being male*. Then, necessarily, the exemplification of *being a bachelor* supervenes on the exemplification of *being unmarried*, *being eligible*, and *being male*.

More generally, the analysis of a property implies that, necessarily, there is a local supervenience base for that property, a base constituted by the ingredients of the analysans. A *local* supervenience base is not meant to be contrasted with an *extrinsic* supervenience base, but rather with a *global* supervenience base. (More on local versus global supervenience in the next chapter.) A property has a local supervenience base if and only if the exemplification of that property by an entity is necessitated by the exemplification of other properties (or relations), whether by that entity itself or by other entities.

The analysis of a property implies that, necessarily, there is a local supervenience base for that property, a base constituted by the ingredients of that property's analysans. In the case of *being a bachelor*, this is quite straightforward. There are three properties in terms of which that property is analysed, and the exemplification of *being a bachelor* by a person is always necessitated by that person's exemplifying those three properties. There are also less straightforward cases. Suppose that *being F* is analysed as *being G* or *being H*. Then if *being F* is exemplified, there is a local supervenience base for that exemplification of *being F*, a base constituted by the ingredients of the analysans—but not always by all the ingredients. For example, the exemplification of *being F* will sometimes locally supervene on just the exemplification of *being G*.[7]

With all this in mind, we can see that, because *being such that there are no hobbits* is not a primitive property of the universe, it must supervene on some of the other properties (relations) exemplified by and in the universe, properties (relations) that are (at least part of) the analysis of *being such that there are no hobbits*. Let the *positive intrinsic character* of the universe comprise all the properties of the universe other than 'lacking' or 'nothing more' or 'totalling' properties, including the properties of having entities within it that themselves have certain properties. So among the properties excluded from the positive intrinsic character are *being such that there are no hobbits* and *being such that there are no non-black ravens*. But also excluded are properties like *being such that there is nothing else* or *being the sum total of everything* or *being the whole universe*.

Now consider a universe much simpler than ours, a universe that is nothing more than—is identical with—a single electron.

---

[7] There might seem to be an exception to the general principle that the analysis of a property implies that, necessarily, there is a local supervenience base for that property. Suppose the analysis of a property can have a 'negative aspect' without a corresponding 'negative property'. For example, suppose *being F** is analysed as being *F* while failing to be *G*. Let us add that what fails to be *G* does not have the property of *failing to be G*. Then consider a world with exactly one object, *O*, whose only accidental properties are *being F* and *being F**. *O*'s being *F* does not necessitate its being *F**. Nevertheless, all of this is consistent with our analysis of *being F**, so none of this implies that *F** is primitive or fundamental. So it looks as if we have a case of a property being 'analysed' that does not involve its supervening on other properties.

This may be how it looks. But I do not think that this is how it is. Suppose we say that there is a property of *being H*. We add that this property is, of necessity, exemplified by all and only those things that are not *G*. We add, further, that there is no such property as *failing to be G*. I think we are then confused. For, given what we have said, 'being H' is just our name for *failing to be G*. Likewise, *being F** appears to me, in the account of the preceding paragraph, to be analysed in terms of *being F* and *failing to be G*. *Being F** therefore does have a local supervenience base, after all.

That entire universe could exist—that is, that electron could exist—*and retain its positive intrinsic character* while failing to be a universe. Moreover, it could exist in a world much like ours, but which includes, among many other things, a hobbit. Thus there is nothing in that universe's positive intrinsic character that precludes the existence of a hobbit. So the exemplifying of that positive intrinsic character is not a supervenience base for *being such that there are no hobbits*. Nevertheless, if that electron were the whole universe, then *that hobbits do not exist* would be true.

So it is possible for there to be a universe in which *that hobbits do not exist* is true even if that universe's positive intrinsic character is such that, possibly, that character is exemplified and other things exist, among them a hobbit. In fact, our own universe is such a universe. Possibly, the positive intrinsic features of our own universe are exemplified by something even if that something is not a universe, even if it is part of a much larger universe, even if that much larger universe includes a hobbit or two. Thus the positive intrinsic character of our universe fails to be a local supervenience base for the property of *being such that there are no hobbits*.

This should not be surprising. After all, if the positive intrinsic character of the universe were a local supervenience base for *being such that there are no hobbits*, then that character would necessitate the exemplification of that property. As a result, that character would itself necessitate all truths necessitated by the exemplification of that property. So that positive intrinsic character, all by itself, would necessitate the truth of *that hobbits do not exist*. So there would have been no reason to introduce *being such that there are no hobbits* in the first place.

At any rate, the universe's positive intrinsic character fails to be a local supervenience base for the property of *being such that there are no hobbits*. But suppose that the universe has not only its positive intrinsic character, but also has the property of *being such that there is nothing more in the universe*. The latter property, along with the universe's positive intrinsic character, would deliver a supervenience base for *being such that there are no hobbits*. For the universe's having its positive intrinsic character plus its having the property of *being such that there is nothing more in the universe* absolutely guarantees that no hobbits exist.

Indeed, the only plausible way to get a local supervenience base for *being such that there are no hobbits* is to have some property (relation) or other along the lines of *being such that there is nothing more in the universe*.[8] And there had better be a local supervenience base for *being such that there are no hobbits*. For recall that if *being such that there are no hobbits* is not primitive, then it has a local supervenience base constituted by the properties to which it is reduced or in terms of which it is analysed.

Being such that there are no hobbits is not primitive. But truthmaker theorists have to proffer at least one 'negative existential' and primitive property, a property such as *being such that there is nothing more in the universe*. This is because *being such that there is nothing more in the universe* fails to supervene on the 'positive' properties exemplified by the universe and its denizens. (It fails for the same reason that *being such that there are no hobbits* fails thus to supervene.) So some 'non-positive' property, some property or other along the lines of

---

[8] That is, this is the only plausible way that will also allow us to conclude that that property is not primitive or fundamental. There are other plausible supervenience bases for that property that clearly do not include the properties that would constitute an analysis of that property. For example, given a property of *being true*, the exemplification of *being such that there are no hobbits* locally supervenes on the exemplification of *being true* by *that hobbits do not exist*.

The work done by the property of *being such that there is nothing more in the universe* could be done by a relation. Consider Armstrong's (1997, 2004) 'totaling relation', which relates all that there is if and only if its relata are all that there is. Note that this relation does not relate its relata to things other than those relata—*ex hypothesi*, there are no other things—yet that relation would not hold among its relata if things other than those relata existed. In this way, the totalling relation resembles a monadic but non-intrinsic property.

being such that there is nothing more in the universe, is not locally supervenient at all. And, as we saw above, a property that fails to be thus supervenient is primitive. So I conclude that not only does Truthmaker commit us to some property or other along the lines of *being such that there is nothing more in the universe*, it says that at least one such property is primitive or fundamental or irreducible.

If there is a property of *being such that there are no hobbits*, it is analysed in terms of, or reduced to, other properties, including *being such that there is nothing more in the universe*. Likewise, the property of *being such that there are no non-black ravens* would be analysed, at least in part, in terms of a property like *being such that there is nothing more in the universe*. And so on for other 'negative existential properties'. They would all be analysed, at least in part, in terms of (some property or other along the lines of) *being such that there is nothing more in the universe*.

Those who postulate properties like *being such that there are no hobbits* are led to postulate *being such that there is nothing more in the universe*. But now we have a new potential truthmaker for *that hobbits do not exist*: the 'totality' state of affairs of *the universe's both having the positive intrinsic character it has and also having the property of being such that there is nothing more in the universe*. Given the totality state, we no longer need the state of *the universe's being such that there are no hobbits*.

Since we no longer need the state of *the universe's being such that there are no hobbits*, we should get rid of that state. This is because that state is a speculative and extravagant posit. Note, in particular, that we still lack a reduction or analysis of that state's constituent property. For even though *being such that there are no hobbits* supervenes on the universe's intrinsic character plus the universe's being such that there is nothing else, the properties of this supervenience base cannot be identified with the properties in terms of which *being such that there are no hobbits* is analysed. This is because, if there really is such a property, it could be exemplified by a universe that has a different positive intrinsic character from our own.

When it comes to being the truthmaker for *that hobbits do not exist*, the totality state supplants *the universe's being such that there are no hobbits*. This is our third reason to deny that *that hobbits do not exist* is made true by *the universe's being such that there are no hobbits*. And the totality state supplants not only *the universe's being such that there are no hobbits*, but also *the universe's being such that there are no non-black ravens*. More generally, the totality state seems to be a truthmaker for all negative existential and general truths. We shall return to the totality state in §IV.

III. Minimal Truthmakers for Negative Existentials

In *A World of States of Affairs* (1997: 200), Armstrong says that the totality state is a truthmaker for all negative and general truths. He repeats this in *Truth and Truthmakers* (2004: 58–59). But in this more recent book he emphasizes 'minimal' truthmakers, which he thinks are 'of quite special importance to metaphysics' (2004: 19).

Armstrong says:

We should at this point take a look at negative existential truths: the non-existence of arctic penguins, the phoenix, unicorns, centaurs and the like that traditionally bedevil and enthral philosophers. It is quite often assumed—even in truthmaking circles—that the whole world is required as truthmakers for these truths. This seems far too pessimistic. The (minimal) truthmaker for <there are no arctic penguins> would seem to be the arctic animals (including whatever is the truthmaker for their being animals and living in the arctic), together with the state of affairs that these are the totality of such animals. Each of the arctic animals is, by its nature, *different* from a penguin, as Plato might have said, so this general state of affairs seems truthmaker enough for this negative existential. In the same way, if we work with the totality of all birds, we eliminate the phoenix. (2004: 75–6)

Let *B* be the sum of all birds. (Pretend such 'sums' really exist.) Armstrong's idea seems to be that the state of affairs of B*'s being the totality of birds* is a minimal truthmaker for *that there is no phoenix*.

Now let B^* be the proper part of *B* that is the sum of all birds larger than a hummingbird. And suppose that a phoenix must be larger than a hummingbird. Then B^**'s being the totality of birds larger than a hummingbird* seems to be a truthmaker for *that there is no phoenix*. This casts doubt on B*'s being the totality of birds'* claim to be a *minimal* truthmaker for that same claim. For Armstrong tells us: 'If T is a minimal truthmaker for P, you cannot subtract anything from T and the remainder still be a truthmaker for P' (2004: 19–20).

Of course, the moral here is not that B^**'s being the totality of birds larger than a hummingbird* is the real minimal truthmaker for *that there is no phoenix*. For assume that a phoenix must not only be larger than a hummingbird, but must also be larger than a sparrow. Let B^{**} be the proper part of both *B* and B^* that is the sum of all birds larger than a sparrow. The state of affairs of B^{**}*'s being the totality of birds larger than a sparrow* is a truthmaker for *that there is no phoenix*. The prospects for a minimal truthmaker here look dim.

It is unclear what Armstrong would say about these objections to his proposed minimal truthmaker for *that there is no phoenix*. It is unclear because he does not spell out in detail how to understand 'subtracting' and 'remainder'. Let me propose a response on his behalf, a way of clarifying 'subtracting' and 'remainder'. Although this response will have its own unhappy result, it has the attractions of both being straightforward and also implying that Armstrong's explicitly proposed minimal truthmakers for certain truths are indeed minimal truthmakers for those truths.

Suppose, in general, that O*'s being* F is a minimal truthmaker for *p* only if there is no proper part of *O*, such that the state of *that proper part of* O*'s being* F is a truthmaker for *p*. Given this supposition, B's *being the totality of birds* turns out to be a minimal truthmaker for *that there is no phoenix* after all. For there is no proper part of *B*—not B^*, not B^{**}—that has the property of *being the totality of birds.* And obviously, if no proper part of *B* has that property, there is no state of affairs constituted by a proper part of *B*'s having that property that makes it true that there is no phoenix.

Given this understanding of minimal truthmakers, B's *being the totality of birds* qualifies as a minimal truthmaker for *that there is no phoenix.* That state is not, however, that truth's only minimal truthmaker. B^*'s *being the totality of birds larger than a hummingbird* also counts as a minimal truthmaker for that truth. So does B^{**}'s *being the totality of birds larger than a sparrow.* And—most importantly—so does the totality state of affairs.

We have already seen that the totality state seems to be a truthmaker for all negative existentials. So it is old news that it seems to be a truthmaker for *that there is no phoenix.* What is new is that that state seems to be a *minimal* truthmaker. For there is no state constituted by a proper part of the universe having the property of *being such that there is nothing more in the universe.* (For no proper part of the universe is such that there is *nothing more* than it in the universe.) And obviously, if there is no such state, no such state is a truthmaker for *that there is no phoenix.*

The totality state seems to be a minimal truthmaker for each and every negative existential truth. This undermines Armstrong's motivation for finding minimal truthmakers for negative existential truths, which was a desire to find something less inclusive, and presumably more intuitive, than the totality state. Moreover, once we have the totality state as a minimal truthmaker, the others seem needless. As in the preceding section, the claim that the totality state is the sole truthmaker for negative existential truths emerges as the best position for a truthmaker theorist.

Further support for this conclusion comes from focusing on the distinctive commitments of the 'many minimal truthmakers' approach. And this further support is independent of my suggestion about how to understand 'subtracting' and 'remainder'. For however we understand the details of Armstrong's definition of a 'minimal truthmaker', Armstrong's examples make it clear that such truthmakers involve properties like *being the totality of birds*.[9] I shall assume that this is not a primitive property. Presumably, the property of *being the totality of birds* is somehow reduced to or analysed in terms of other properties. So I assume that its exemplification supervenes on the exemplification of other properties.

Suppose that the object that has the property of *being the totality of birds* is the sum of all birds. That sum has a certain intrinsic character. But that intrinsic character is not sufficient for that sum's having the 'bird totality' property. Rather, that sum's having the 'bird totality' property supervenes on that sum's own positive intrinsic character plus the rest of the universe's positive intrinsic character *plus* the universe's having the property of *being such that there is nothing more in the universe*.

Thus the minimal truthmaker here can do its work only by a combination of intrinsic and extrinsic properties, properties that seem to supervene on the entire positive intrinsic character of the universe plus the universe's having the property of *being such that there is nothing more in the universe*. In general, minimal truthmakers lead us to the totality state, which state can do

---

[9] The objections raised in the previous section to properties like *being such that there are no hobbits* apply to Armstrong's *being the totality of birds*. First, *that there is no phoenix* does not seem to be about the sum of birds $b_1 \ldots b_n$ exemplifying a property, not even a 'bird totality' property. Second, *being the totality of birds* is arguably suspicious; and to insist that it is not is to give the cheater leave to introduce her own special properties, tailor-made to accommodate Truthmaker. The third objection assumes that *being the totality of birds* is not a primitive property and is developed in the text. If that property is primitive, on the other hand, then it would surely be suspicious, and the whole enterprise of even more aid and comfort to cheaters.

their truthmaking work all on its own. We have no need of states like B's *being the totality of birds* and the ontological commitments they incur.[10]

IV. The Totality State of Affairs

Bertrand Russell (1985) says that there is a totality state.[11] David Armstrong (1997: 200–1) does as well, saying explicitly that it

[10] Suppose we replace *being the totality of birds* with an *alling* relation, which holds between birds, necessarily, if and only if they are all the birds that exist. Another *alling* relation holds between all the animals if and only if they are all the animals that exist. Having different relata, these must be different relations. More generally, there will be as many *alling* relations as there are minimal truthmakers. Lest we have a wide variety of primitive *alling* relations corresponding to the wide variety of negative existentials, these will have to be analysed. The analysis of most elegance invokes, among other things, a single *alling simpliciter* relation relating each existing entity to every other existing entity.

Another option depends on a primitive relation R that, necessarily, relates all entities with *being F* if and only if those entities are all the Fs. So, e.g., necessarily, that relation relates birds $b_1 \ldots b_n$ with the property of *being a bird* if and only if $b_1 \ldots b_n$ are all the birds. This relation R gives us a totality state, since, necessarily, R relates all existing entities $e_1 \ldots e_n$ with the property of (say) *being self-identical* if and only if they are all the self-identical (and so all the existing) entities. This totality state will be a truthmaker for *that there is no phoenix*. So will the state constituted by $R, b_1 \ldots b_n$, and *being a bird*. But this latter truthmaker does not seem to be of 'quite special importance for metaphysics'; i.e., it seems no more important than the totality state; note, in particular, that it has the same constituent relation—R—as the totality state. Moreover, once we have the totality state, the other instances of R follow of necessity. All of this suggests that we make the totality state our focus.

[11] Russell says: 'It is perfectly clear, I think, that when you have enumerated all the atomic facts in the world, it is a further fact about the world that those are all the atomic facts there are about the world, and that is just as much an objective fact about the world as any of them are' (1985: 103). But he goes on to say: 'The same thing applies to "All men are mortal". When you have taken all the particular men that there are, and found each one of them severally to be mortal, it is definitely a new fact that all men are mortal; how new a fact, appears from what I said a moment ago, that it could not be inferred from the mortality of the several men that there are in the world' (1985: 103; see also Russell 1919: 6). So Russell endorses both the totality state and also sundry general facts, such as the fact that all men are mortal. This looks like overkill, given that the totality state alone seems to do all the truthmaking that needs to be done.

is the truthmaker for all negative existential truths. And I agree, in light of the last two sections, that the truthmaker theorist should take the totality state to be the truthmaker for all negative existential truths and all general truths. That is, I agree that this is the truthmaker theorist's least bad option. Nevertheless, I have five objections to taking the totality state to be the truthmaker for all negative existential and general truths.

Suppose that the totality state were the truthmaker for negative existential truths. Then the primitive property of *being such that there is nothing more in the universe* would not be suspicious (see Ch. 2, §IV). But I object that it *is* suspicious. And I am not alone. Here is Theodore Sider on what makes a property suspicious:

> What seems common to all the cheats is that irreducibly hypothetical properties are postulated [in providing truthmakers], whereas a proper ontology should invoke only *categorical*, or occurrent, properties and relations. Categorical properties involve what objects are actually like, whereas hypothetical properties 'point beyond' their instances. (2001: 41)

Among the sorts of properties that Sider deems to be hypothetical, and so suspicious, are properties like *being such that the Trojans were conquered* (Sider 2001: 40–1).

Even given my somewhat hazy understanding of 'pointing beyond' their instances, I can sometimes recognize cases of such pointing. And I recognize it in properties like *being such that there is nothing more in the universe*. These properties are 'hypothetical' in Sider's intended sense. So Sider—who is a fellow-traveller with truthmaker theorists—should join me in charging that a 'nothing more' property is suspicious.[12]

Of course, the dedicated truthmaker theorist will deny that *being such that there is nothing more in the universe* is suspicious.

---

[12] I do not endorse Sider's criterion for what makes a property suspicious. For I deny that all modal properties are suspicious (see Ch. 5). But Sider (2001: 40–1) explicitly says that such properties are 'hypothetical', and so suspicious.

Similarly, the dedicated Lucretian will deny that *being such that the Trojans were conquered* is suspicious (Ch. 2, §IV; Ch. 6, §III). Nevertheless, it is perfectly respectable to object to Lucretianism simply because its properties strike one as suspicious. Likewise, it is perfectly respectable to object to the totality state simply because primitive 'nothing more' properties seem to be suspicious. This is the first objection to the totality state as a truthmaker for all negative existential and general truths.

When it comes to resisting cheaters, I suppose that it is better to have postulated exactly one conjured-up-to-meet-the-demands-of-Truthmaker-but-otherwise-undreamt-of property than to have postulated many. But the truthmaker theorist who postulates even one such property cannot say that all such special properties are suspicious, which makes it difficult to resist other such properties in a principled way.

For example, consider the presentist who postulates the property of *having a past that was exhaustively thus and so*. This presentist can say that the state of the universe's having that property is a truthmaker for every truth about the past, and can thus appease Truthmaker. Truthmaker theorists will have a hard time objecting, in a principled way, to that property if they have themselves postulated a primitive 'nothing more' property simply to appease Truthmaker. In this way, the totality property weakens Truthmaker's ability to catch cheaters. This is the second objection.

The third objection asks us to imagine a world with two electrons, *E* and E^*. Add that *E* has the property of *being such that there is an electron other than* E. I say that the state of *E*'s having that property is not the truthmaker for *that an electron other than* E *exists*. The truthmaker is, instead, E^*. For the existence of E^* is why *that an electron other than* E *exists* is true. Indeed, it is why *E* has the property of *being such that there is an electron other than* E.

Likewise, I think that the existence of the state of the universe's having the property of *being such that there is nothing more in the universe* does not explain why *that there is nothing more in the universe* is true. Again, that claim is not true because that state exists. Rather, that claim is true because nothing more exists. And it is because there is nothing more that the universe has the property of *being such that there is nothing more in the universe*, if it really does have that property. As a result, I conclude that the state of the universe's having that 'nothing more' property does not make it true that there is nothing more. So it does not make it true that there are neither hobbits nor white ravens.

The fourth objection begins by noting that the totality state of affairs is supposed to be the truthmaker for:

(1) Hobbits do not exist.

That state is also supposed to be the truthmaker for *that all ravens are black*. It follows from this that (1)'s truthmaker could not exist if there were white ravens. Similarly, that truthmaker—since it is supposed to be the truthmaker for all negative existential truths—could not exist if there were golden mountains; it could not exist if there were flying pigs; it could not exist if there were talking donkeys. Moreover, *that there are exactly n black ravens* has a 'negative aspect', and so its truthmaker is (1)'s truthmaker: the totality state of affairs. So the totality state could not exist if we eliminated one raven.

Because of the truthmaking work it does, the totality state could not exist if any object or state or entity existed that does not actually exist. Nor could the totality state exist if any actual existent failed to exist. Truthmaker implies that if a property is exemplified, there is the state of affairs of that property's being exemplified (Ch. 2, §I). So it implies that we add or subtract the exemplification of a property only by thereby adding or subtracting the existence of a state of affairs.

So, given Truthmaker, the totality state could not exist if any property that is exemplified were not exemplified or any property that is not exemplified were. It could not exist if any entity existed that does not or any entity did not exist that does. But I object that *that all ravens are black* is not *about* a state like that. *That all ravens are black* is not about something that could not possibly exist if (for example) I had worn a red shirt when in fact I wore a blue one. So *that all ravens are black* is not about the totality state. Nor are the other general truths about that state. Nor are negative existential truths.

Further support for this objection comes from noting that, in light of the previous paragraph's remarks, the totality state is, arguably, a world-bound individual. Arguably, the totality state exists only in worlds (i.e., the actual world) in which every actual truth is true. Like every other actual world-bound individual, it necessitates every truth. But, as we saw in Chapter 2 (§III), not every world-bound individual is a truthmaker for every truth and, relatedly, not every truth is appropriately about every world-bound individual. By the same reasoning, not every world-bound individual is a truthmaker for every negative existential and general truth. And I say that the totality state is no better a candidate for being the truthmaker for all negative existential and general truths than is any other world-bound individual. This completes the fourth objection.

Recall that *Fido's being brown* must have its constituents essentially to be the truthmaker for *that Fido is brown*. That this event has both Fido and *being brown* essentially may not be particularly controversial. But now suppose that World War II was an event. That is, suppose that that war was a complex state of affairs constituted by many objects and many properties and many events, including, among others, all the firings of all the weapons that occurred in the service of the war.

I think that that event does not have all of its constituents essentially. For it seems that that war would have existed even if, for example, some soldier had failed to fire his weapon on one occasion when he actually did fire it. Similarly, I deny that the totality state—which is far more complex than any war—has all of its constituents essentially. Yet one moral of the points made in developing the fourth objection above is that the totality state does its truthmaking work only if it has all of its constituents essentially. This is the fifth objection.

A more modest version of this fifth objection begins by pointing out that the essential constituents of even familiar and mundane entities are a matter of controversy. This goes not only for events like World War II, but also for objects like lumps of clay and statues. Given this, so the objection goes, we should admit that we do not know which constituents of the totality state are essential. In particular, we do not know that the totality state has every last one of its constituents essentially. So we should not assert that it does. And so we should not assert that the totality state is the truthmaker for all negative existential and general truths.

V. Objections to Truthmaker

The best truthmaker for a negative existential truth is the single totality state of affairs (§§II–III). But even this 'best truthmaker' is subject to serious objections (§IV). And objections to Truthmaker's handling of negative existential truths are objections to Truthmaker itself. For Truthmaker says that all truths—including negative existential truths—have truthmakers (§I).

That there are not plausible truthmakers for negative existential truths is a reason to reject Truthmaker. Moreover, that Truthmaker demands that negative existential truths have truthmakers in the first place is itself a reason to reject Truthmaker. For it is implausible that a claim asserting that a thing *fails to exist* is made true by—and so is appropriately about—some other, *existing* thing. So I say that negative existentials do not have truthmakers, and that Truthmaker is therefore false.

Roy Sorensen (2001: 171–80) claims that only truths that have truthmakers can be known. So one might object that, since we do in fact know many negative existentials, they must have truthmakers. But Sorensen's claim, and thus the objection predicated on it, is mistaken. It is false that truthmakerless truths are (or would be) unknowable.

To begin to see why I say this, suppose, for the sake of argument, that negative existentials do have truthmakers. Suppose, further, that they have the best (least bad) truthmaker, the totality state. So, let us suppose, the totality state is the truthmaker for *that there is no rhinoceros in this room*. Even so, I never rely on that totality state—I do not perceive it or intuit it or enjoy some other acquaintance with it—in coming to know that there is no rhinoceros in this room.

Rather, I know that there is no rhinoceros in this room, at least in part, because if there were a rhinoceros in this room, I would easily perceive it. So I casually glance about, fail to perceive any rhinoceros, and rightly conclude that this room is rhinoceros-free. The totality state plays no role in any of this. Even if that state exists, it is epistemically irrelevant.

Besides, the (false) claim that I come to know a negative existential by somehow being acquainted with its truthmaker seems to have the absurd result that all negative existentials—in virtue of having the same truthmaker, the totality state—are epistemically on a par. But of course they are not. Again, I can know the truth of *that there is no rhinoceros in this room* by casually glancing about, or perhaps even by carefully sniffing. But I cannot thus come to know the truth of *that there is no virus V in this room*.[13]

---

[13] Similar remarks apply if we abandon the idea that the totality state is a truthmaker for all negative existentials, and instead say that each negative existential has its own tailor-made truthmaker. Suppose that one of the above negative existentials is made true by the state of *the universe's being such that there is no rhinoceros in this room* and the other by the state of *the universe's being such*

In general, even if there were truthmakers for negative existential truths, those truthmakers would be irrelevant to our coming to know those truths. So negative existentials' lacking truthmakers would not make them any harder to know. I have argued that negative existentials lack truthmakers. And of course we know some negative existentials. So I conclude that we know some truthmakerless truths.[14]

This chapter has focused on negative existentials. For Truthmaker's demand that every truth is made true by the mere existence of something is most strikingly perverse when it comes to claims about what does not exist. But, to push a point broached in Chapter 2 (§I), I think it is implausible for other sorts of claims as well.

Consider the 'theory' that the whole world is a single ball, which goes from being red to being white. Truthmaker says that this theory is committed to the existence of one thing (the truthmaker for *that the ball is red*) followed by the existence of another (the truthmaker for *that the ball is white*). Indeed, Truthmaker also implies that something exists which makes it true that the second thing follows the first. Moreover, according to Truthmaker, these truthmakers are what this theory of the world is about. But none of what Truthmaker implies about this theory is plausible.

Truthmaker claims that each and every possible truth is—in Truthmaker's relational sense of 'about'—about the positive existence of this or that. This claim is implausible, and not

---

that there is no virus V in this room. These two states are epistemically on a par, equally hidden from my prying eyes.

[14] This undermines the second premiss of one of Sorensen's (2001: 165 ff.) defences of epistemicism with regard to vagueness. That defence's premisses are, first, that truths about borderline cases are truths without truthmakers, and, second, that those truths are unknowable because they lack truthmakers.

merely because of negative existential truths. So I reject Truthmaker. And I suggest we now turn to Truthmaker's cousin, Truth Supervenes on Being. For, as we shall see, Truth Supervenes on Being seems to satisfy what motivates Truthmaker without implying that every truth is about what positively exists.

4

TRUTH SUPERVENES ON BEING

Truth Supervenes on Being (TSB) says that any two possible worlds alike with respect to both what entities exist and which properties (and relations) each of those entities exemplifies are thereby alike with respect to what is true. Ludwig Wittgenstein's *Tractatus* defends something closer to TSB than to Truthmaker.[1] And David Lewis (2001), among others, explicitly defends TSB.

As we shall see, TSB appears both to articulate the idea that truth depends substantively on being and also to avoid Truthmaker's worst consequences. But this chapter argues that, despite appearances to the contrary, TSB does not really articulate the idea that truth depends substantively on being. This chapter then reformulates TSB so that it does articulate that idea. This reformulated TSB ends up being little better than Truthmaker.

---

[1] Wittgenstein (1961: 4.25) says that elementary truths—true propositions that are not reducible to other propositions and logical operators—are true because of something's existence. So he seems to say that elementary truths have truthmakers. But he does not defend Truthmaker, since he does not think that all truths have truthmakers. For example, he does not think that the true denial of an elementary proposition has a truthmaker, since that denial is not true because of the existence of anything. Instead, according to Wittgenstein, that denial is true because of the falsity of the denied elementary proposition, which is false because a certain state of affairs does not to exist.

I. Apparent Advantages of TSB over Truthmaker

Advantage 1

TSB seems to articulate a way for truth to depend on being. And the dependence that TSB articulates is non-trivial, since some views violate it. For example, according to Lewis (1999*a*), both Ryle's account of dispositions and also presentism violate TSB. Theodore Sider (2001: 40–1) agrees that these views are TSB-transgressing cheaters, adding that the same goes for the view that there are true 'brute counterfactuals'.[2]

Since TSB articulates a non-trivial way for truth to depend on being, it thereby seems to accommodate Truthmaker's primary motivation, which is the insight or idea or intuition that all truth depends substantively on being (Ch. 1, §I).[3] Indeed, TSB seems to fit with that primary motivation better than does Truthmaker itself. For, as I shall now argue, unlike Truthmaker, TSB does not demand more than is required by truth's dependence on being or, relatedly, more than is needed to catch cheaters.

We saw in Chapter 2 (§I) that Truthmaker outstrips its primary motivation. For example, when it comes to the truth of *that Fido is brown*, that motivation seems to demand only a brown Fido. But Truthmaker demands more. Truthmaker demands both that a state of affairs along the lines of *Fido's being brown* exists and also that this state has its constituents essentially. Relatedly, Truthmaker wrongly implies that those

---

[2] Both Ryle's account of dispositions and also 'brute counterfactuals' are discussed in Ch. 7. Presentism is addressed in §III below and, in more detail, in Ch. 6. Sider correctly says that TSB catches these cheaters only if it refuses to admit certain properties into the supervenience base. As I shall note in §VI, TSB, no less than Truthmaker, must deem some properties to be suspicious if it is to catch cheaters.

[3] Some endorse Truthmaker because they take it to be the correspondence theory of truth (Ch. 1, §I). But it is not that theory (Ch. 1, §IV; Ch. 2, §IV). Neither is TSB.

who believe in a brown Fido, but not in states of affairs, cheat when they say that *that Fido is brown* is true.

TSB, on the other hand, says that Fido's existing and being brown are enough to ground the truth of *that Fido is brown*. This is because, just so long as our world includes a brown Fido, *that Fido is brown* is true in every world like ours with respect to which entities exist and which properties each of those entities exemplifies. Along similar lines, according to TSB, those who say that *that Fido is brown* is true do not cheat just so long as they believe in a brown Fido.

Advantage 2

Truthmaker says that each truth has a truthmaker. So it says that each negative existential truth has a truthmaker. But even the best account of the truthmaker for a negative existential is subject to serious objections (Ch. 3, §IV). Besides, if a negative existential had a truthmaker, then that negative existential would both be necessitated by and also be about its truthmaker. So by saying that each negative existential has a truthmaker, Truthmaker implies that each negative existential is necessitated by, and is about, what positively exists. But this implication is false (Ch. 3, §V).

TSB does not imply that any negative existential is necessitated by the positive existence of something. Nor does it imply that each negative existential is somehow about the positive existence of something. In fact, TSB has none of Truthmaker's false implications regarding negative existentials. Instead, TSB implies only that if a negative existential is true, then that same negative existential is true in all possible worlds exactly like ours with respect to which entities exist and which properties those entities have.

Advantage 3

Consider a possible world W_1 that includes a contingently existing object X. Presumably, there is a world W_2, differing with respect to what exists from W_1 only in that W_2 does not include X. One might quibble: what if some objects are essentially parts of X? Then W_2 lacks them as well. What if some objects have X essentially as a part? Then they too are absent from W_2. Even the quibblers should grant that, with respect to what exists, there is a world W_2 that differs from W_1 *only* in that W_2 lacks some of the inhabitants of W_1.

But, as David Lewis (2001) points out, truthmaker theorists cannot grant this. In W_2 it is true that X does not exist. According to Truthmaker, something must exist in W_2—call it 'Y'—that makes it true that X does not exist. Y, since it makes it true that X does not exist, cannot possibly exist in a world with X. So, while Y must exist in W_2, it cannot exist in W_1. Thus Truthmaker says that we can remove X only by replacing it with Y (or with some other truthmaker for *that* X *does not exist*).

Truthmaker makes it impossible simply to remove an entity. One must always replace it with something else: namely, a truthmaker for the claim that that entity does not exist. But what Truthmaker says is impossible seems to be possible. This is a cost of Truthmaker.

TSB allows that two worlds can differ only by one of them lacking some of the inhabitants of the other. In other words, TSB allows that one world can contain all the inhabitants of another world, plus some extra things besides. So TSB does not have the cost of Truthmaker just noted. This is TSB's third advantage over Truthmaker.

II. Global versus 'Worldwide Local' Supervenience

TSB is a thesis of *global* supervenience. Lewis endorses this thesis of global supervenience when he tells us: 'For any proposition P and any worlds W and V, if P is true in W but not in V, then either something exists in one of the worlds but not in the other, or else some n-tuple of things stands in some fundamental relation in one of the worlds but not in the other' (2001: 612).[4] Lewis also says:

There is a most inclusive subject matter: *being*. Differences in being come in two sorts. There are differences in whether something is, and there are differences in how something is. Two worlds are alike with respect to being if they have no differences of either sort.... And every proposition, no matter what lesser subject matter it may have, is entirely about being. It never has different truth values in two worlds that are just alike with respect to being. In John Bigelow's (1988: 132–3) phrase 'its truth is supervenient on being'. (2003: 25–6)

And here is Theodore Sider describing how TSB bears on a negative existential:

[TSB] does not require the existence of a fact that there are no unicorns; it merely requires that since 'there are no unicorns' is true in the actual world, it must also be true in any world in which the same objects exist, those objects instantiate the same properties, and those objects stand in the same relations as they do in the actual world. (2001: 36)

Clearly, TSB's defenders take it to be a thesis of global supervenience.

But, as we shall see below, these same defenders sometimes treat TSB as if it were a thesis of a different sort. They sometimes treat TSB as if it were the claim that truth *locally supervenes on the whole of reality*. Understood in this way, TSB says that, necessarily, each true claim is such that, necessarily,

---

[4] Lewis says that truth globally supervenes on what exists and which *fundamental* properties (relations) those existents exemplify. But I said that TSB is the claim that truth globally supervenes on what exists and which properties (relations) those things exemplify, without the qualification of 'fundamental'. No matter. Suppose every property is either fundamental or reducible to (analysed in terms of) fundamental properties; then my account of TSB entails Lewis's, and vice versa; so the difference between the accounts is irrelevant to the points raised here. These accounts fail to entail each other only if, possibly, some properties are analysed in terms of others *ad infinitum*, never bottoming out in fundamental properties; if this is indeed possible, then my formulation of TSB is less objectionable than Lewis's.

given all the entities that exist and the properties that each of those entities has, then that claim is true. Equivalently, TSB taken as a thesis of 'worldwide local supervenience' tells us that, necessarily, no true claim could possibly fail to be true given what exists and the properties had by each thing.

Worldwide local TSB, unlike global TSB, is defined without reference to possible worlds. (This is important, as we shall see in §§III and V below.) Nevertheless, assuming that there are possible worlds, worldwide local TSB is true if and only if the following claim about possible worlds is true: No matter which world is actual, every actual truth is true in all worlds in which (at least) every actual object exists and in which every such object has (at least) all the properties it actually has.

The following illustrates the substantive difference between worldwide local TSB and global TSB. Suppose, for the sake of this example, that there is nothing like a 'nothing more' property. Then, possibly, every actual object exists, and each such object exemplifies every property that it actually exemplifies, and there also exists a unicorn. This possibility rules out worldwide local TSB, since it implies that the truth of *that unicorns do not exist*, which is actually true, fails to supervene locally on all the actually existing objects and their having the properties they actually have. But this possibility is consistent with global TSB. For this possibility does not imply that worlds alike with respect to what exists (and with respect to which properties those existents exemplify) differ with respect to the truth of *that unicorns do not exist.*[5]

Global supervenience is one thing, worldwide local supervenience another. Should we take TSB as a thesis of global supervenience or, instead, as a thesis of worldwide local supervenience? The question here is not which version of TSB Lewis

---

[5] We have just considered an example involving a truth that, given that there is nothing like a 'nothing more' property, satisfies global TSB but not worldwide local TSB. Below we shall see that there are truths that, given presentism, satisfy worldwide local TSB but not global TSB.

or Sider prefers. (I think that both clearly prefer the global version.) Rather, I am asking which version of TSB better articulates the idea that truth depends on being. Relatedly, I am asking which version is better at catching cheaters. That is, I am asking which version of TSB accommodates Truthmaker's motivations.

Recall that I am turning to TSB not merely because it avoids some of Truthmaker's unpalatable commitments. (Lots of views do that, including the simple denial of Truthmaker.) I am turning to TSB because it also appears to articulate the idea that truth depends substantively on being. And, as we shall see in each of the following four sections, only TSB taken as a thesis of worldwide local supervenience really does articulate that idea. Only when taken as a thesis of worldwide local supervenience can TSB serve as an alternative to Truthmaker for those who think that truth substantively depends on being—and so think that to violate that dependence is to cheat—but who do not wish to endorse Truthmaker itself.

III. TSB and Presentism

TSB's defenders allege that presentism cheats (Lewis 1999*a*; Sider 2001: ch. 2). This alone suggests that TSB should be understood as a thesis of worldwide local supervenience. For, I shall argue, only thus understood does TSB have a shot at catching presentism.

The first step of that argument explains how presentism bears on the nature of possible worlds. (More on presentism in Ch. 6.) Presentists say that the whole of being comprises that which exists at the present time alone. Since no dinosaurs exist at the present time, presentists say that there simply are no dinosaurs. So they say that *that there are dinosaurs* is false. But palaeontologically informed presentists add that *that there are dinosaurs* was once true. Thus presentism implies that propositions can change in truth-value.[6] As we shall see, this implication of presentism conflicts with a standard account of possible worlds.

Most philosophers who embrace possible worlds deny that they are universes like our own. Rather, these philosophers take possible worlds to be abstract representations of some sort. So let us assume that possible worlds are abstract representations. Indeed, let us assume that they are abstract propositions.

A proposition *p* is maximal if and only if, for every proposition *q*, *p* entails *q*, or, instead, *p* entails *q*'s denial. With this in mind, consider this account of possible worlds. A possible world is a possibly true *maximal* proposition. This account of possible worlds also identifies a world's *being actual* with that world's *being true*. Thus it tells us that the *actual world* is nothing other than the true maximal proposition.[7]

Given presentism, the true maximal proposition entails the denial of *that there are dinosaurs*. But since there were dinosaurs, presentists must say that the true maximal proposition has not always been true. This implies, given the above account of possible worlds, that the actual world has not always been actual. But that implication is not acceptable. For which world is actual does not change from moment to moment. Besides, as we shall see in Chapter 6 (§II), presentists have a role for

---

[6] In contrast, the *eternalist* says that the whole of being comprises the past, present, and future. Past times and future times are not 'now', but they are real. This is analogous, says the eternalist, to distant places failing to be 'here', yet being real. Since the past includes dinosaurs, the eternalist says that—although no dinosaurs are located at the present time—dinosaurs do exist. Thus the eternalist says that *that there are dinosaurs* is true. As I argue in Merricks 2006, I think that eternalism and presentism are the only live options. So at one point in this section, I shall assume that all non-presentists (since they should be eternalists) should say that no propositions change their truth-value.

[7] This is Plantinga's account from *The Nature of Necessity*, except that I identify abstract 'states of affairs' (such as *Fido's being brown*, which exists whether or not it obtains) with abstract propositions (such as *that Fido is brown*) and *obtaining* with *being true*, whereas Plantinga (1974: 45; 1987: 192) neither rejects nor endorses these identifications.

maximal propositions to play other than that of possible worlds. Presentists should take maximal propositions to be 'abstract times'.[8]

Presentists should come up with a variation on the above account of possible worlds that works with their view of time. Specifically, presentists should define a 'possible world' as a possibly true proposition that is maximal *with respect to propositions that never change their truth-value*.[9]

---

[8] Some might object that presentists should take both times and worlds to be abstract maximal propositions; i.e., that presentists should identify abstract times with possible worlds. I reply that possible worlds and abstract times are technical devices to serve our prior notions of modality and temporality. And I deny that those prior notions permit the conflation of temporality and modality that would follow from identifying times with worlds.

One difference between temporality and modality that might be obscured if we identified times with worlds is the difference between a 'temporal' conditional and a subjunctive conditional. This temporal conditional is clearly true: when there were dinosaurs, there were no humans. But this subjunctive conditional, while perhaps true, is surely not clearly so: if there were dinosaurs, there would be no humans. (Perhaps if there were dinosaurs, there would be a scientist who cloned dinosaurs from DNA trapped in amber.)

Another objection concedes that times are one thing, worlds another. But it claims that times alike with respect to both what exists and also which properties those existents exemplify are thereby alike with respect to what is true. Presentists should simply reject this claim. Moreover, the eternalist should reject this claim as well. For, if the underlying idea here that times alike with respect to being are alike with respect to truth really is distinct from global TSB, the eternalist must read this claim as saying that times alike with respect to what is located at those times, and with respect to what properties which things have while located at those times, are alike with respect to what is true. But the eternalist denies that times thus alike 'in being' must be alike with respect to what is true. Two times in two worlds could be thus alike 'in being' even if the futures of those worlds diverge, so that some of what is true (about the future) at one of those times differs from what is true (about the future) at the other.

[9] Rather than figure out a presentist-friendly account of worlds, some might just reject possible worlds altogether. But to dismiss possible worlds is thereby to dismiss global TSB itself. For global TSB must be defined in terms of possible worlds. To give global TSB a fighting chance, assume that good sense can be made of possible worlds.

Another reaction is to reject presentism because it cannot be reconciled with one's favoured account of worlds. But this reaction, no less than the previous one, undermines the global TSB-based objection to presentism. That objection

Those who define possible worlds in terms of fully maximal propositions typically presuppose that propositions never change their truth-value. As a result, they conflate fully maximal propositions with propositions that are maximal only with respect to propositions that never change their truth-value. Indeed, because presentists alone should say that some propositions change their truth-value, non-presentists should see this 'conflation' as a correct identification. Thus non-presentists, no less than presentists, should accept the above presentist-friendly definition of 'possible world'.

Every believer in abstract possible worlds should accept that definition. Or, a bit more cautiously, every believer should insist that the propositions that are 'true in' an abstract world never change their truth-value. And they should say this whether they think that a possible world is itself a proposition or instead some other abstract representation. (More on what abstract possible worlds might be in Ch. 5, §II.) Any such account of abstract worlds will underwrite the argument of this section, even though my exposition of that argument will focus on possible worlds as propositions.

So let us say that possible worlds are themselves propositions, propositions that are maximal with respect to propositions that never change their truth-value. Then—if presentism is true—the actual world does not entail *that there are dinosaurs*, nor does it entail *that it is not the case that there are dinosaurs*. Instead, it entails *that dinosaurs exist at time t, that it is not the case that dinosaurs exist at t**, and so on. (See Plantinga 1985: 90–1; 1987: 192.)

The actual world was actual (true) a thousand years ago. But, given presentism, *that Merricks exists* was not true a thousand years ago. So, given presentism, the actual world does not

---

says that, assuming presentism for *reductio*, there are truths that do not globally supervene on being. That objection simply fails if, assuming presentism for *reductio*, we can make no sense of possible worlds or global supervenience.

entail *that Merricks exists*. This means that, given presentism, *that Merricks exists* is not 'true in' the actual world. For a claim *p*'s being 'true in a world *w*' just is *p*'s being such that, necessarily, if *w* were actual (that is, true), then *p* would be true.

That Merricks exists is true. But, given presentism, it is not true in the actual world. Since it is not true in the actual world, obviously it is not true in all worlds like the actual world with respect to what exists and which properties those existents exemplify. As a result, given presentism, *that Merricks exists* fails to supervene globally on what exists and which properties those existents exemplify.

This result, as we shall see, is the downfall of the global TSB-based objection to presentism. That objection has two premises. The first is that, assuming presentism for *reductio*, global TSB is violated. The second is that, again assuming presentism for *reductio*, a violation of global TSB is thereby a violation of truth's dependence on being. The above result shows that this second premiss is false.

It shows this because, given my existence, the truth of *that Merricks exists* surely depends on being. Given my existence, that truth even has a truthmaker: me. But we have just seen that, assuming presentism, that truth does not satisfy global TSB, not even if I exist. Thus, assuming presentism, a truth can violate global TSB even if that truth depends on being. So, assuming presentism, global TSB fails to articulate truth's dependence on being. Thus the global TSB-based objection to presentism fails.

But there is a more promising catch-the-cheaters-style objection to presentism in the neighbourhood. That objection begins by noting that it is false that, necessarily, if each of the presently existing objects exists and exemplifies every property it presently exemplifies, then *that the Trojans were conquered* is true. It begins by noting, in other words, that the truth of *that the Trojans were conquered* does not *supervene locally* on all the objects that exist at the present time and on all the properties that each such object presently exemplifies. According to presentism, the presently existing objects and their presently exemplified properties are all the objects and all the exemplified properties. So, given presentism, *that the Trojans were conquered* does not supervene locally on all the objects that exist and on all the properties exemplified by those objects. But, so this objection goes, all truths should thus supervene. So presentism is false.

This objection sidesteps presentism's bearing on modal metaphysics. For this objection is not in terms of global supervenience, but in terms of worldwide local supervenience. Moreover, I think that this is the TSB-style objection to presentism actually raised by Lewis and Sider. Thus Lewis objects: '[Presentism] says that although there is nothing outside the present, yet there are past-tensed and future-tensed truths that do not supervene on the present, and hence do not supervene on being' (1999*a*: 207). And Sider says: '...what is true supervenes on what objects exist, what properties those objects have, and what relations they stand in .... For the presentist, all states of affairs are *currently* existing states of affairs, and the properties and relations of objects are confined to those of *currently* existing objects. But surely the truth of the past is not fixed by such facts about the present' (2001: 36–7). The most straightforward way to read Lewis and Sider here is as objecting that presentism violates (what I have called) worldwide local TSB. Taking this straightforward reading as the correct reading, I said earlier that Lewis and Sider sometimes seem to treat TSB as a thesis of worldwide local supervenience.[10]

---

[10] Some might object that a 'less straightforward' reading is more charitable, a reading that interprets the above comments of Lewis and Sider as raising an objection in terms of global supervenience. But in presenting the objection under discussion, Lewis and Sider completely ignore both presentism's bearing on the nature of possible worlds and also presentism's bearing on the formulation of global supervenience. This would be an unacceptable oversight if their objection really did rely on global TSB. And attributing such an oversight to them seems

Many of presentism's opponents take it to be a paradigmatic cheater. But, as we have seen, TSB has a shot at 'catching' presentism only if TSB is a thesis of worldwide local supervenience. So we should take TSB as a thesis of worldwide local supervenience. And we should set global TSB aside.

We saw above that, given presentism, global TSB fails to articulate the idea that truth depends on being. But whether global TSB successfully articulates the *idea* that truth depends on being is a purely conceptual matter. So, whether global TSB thus succeeds should not vary with this or that feature of the cosmos, including the nature of time. Since global TSB fails to articulate that idea given presentism, we should conclude that global TSB simply fails to articulate that idea. Again, we should set global TSB aside.

IV. TSB and Negative Existentials

When it comes to the dependence of truth on being, it is trivial that worlds alike with respect to *what exists* are alike with respect to *truths and falsehoods about what exists*. For example, it is trivial that worlds alike with respect to what exists are alike with respect to the falsity of *that unicorns exist*.[11] Moreover, it is trivial that worlds alike with respect to the falsity of *that*

---

to me unduly uncharitable. Besides, there does not seem to be any such oversight at all, since their objections to presentism seem, again, to rely on worldwide local TSB.

[11] This assumes that *being a unicorn* must be had essentially. But suppose that *being a unicorn* can be exemplified accidentally. Even so, it is still trivial that worlds alike with respect to what exists *and which properties those existents exemplify* are alike with respect to the falsity of *that unicorns exist*. This is enough for the argument to follow, which trades on the point that TSB—a claim about worlds alike both in what exists and also in which properties those existents exemplify—does not articulate a non-trivial way for the truth of *that unicorns do not exist* to depend on being.

unicorns exist are alike with respect to the truth of *that unicorns do not exist*. So we can conclude that it is trivial that worlds alike with respect to what exists are alike with respect to the truth of *that unicorns do not exist*. More generally, it is trivial that worlds alike with respect to what exists are alike with respect to the truth of negative existentials.

This implies that everything that global TSB has to say about the dependence of the truth of negative existentials on being is trivial. For example, when it comes to *that unicorns do not exist*, global TSB says *only* that worlds alike with respect to what exists (and alike with respect to the properties of those existents) are alike with respect to the truth of *that unicorns do not exist*. The same goes for what global TSB says about the truth of any negative existential.

All that global TSB says about the dependence of negative existential truths on being is trivial. I shall now argue that global TSB's triviality in this regard is problematic. I begin by criticizing part of Lewis's reply to an objection by truthmaker theorist C. B. Martin. Here is Lewis:

Martin has noted that when I say that a negative existential truth is true for lack of falsemakers, my statement that there are no falsemakers is itself a negative existential (Martin, 1996, p. 61). Sometimes, in fact, as in the case of the proposition that there are no unicorns, it is the very same negative existential. So the proposition that there are no unicorns is true just because there are no unicorns! What sort of explanation is that?—No explanation at all, I agree. But who says a Truthmaker Principle, whether weakened or not, must yield informative explanations? I say to Martin: *Tu quoque!* His original, full-strength Truthmaker Principle says that a positive existential, for instance the proposition that there is a cat, is true because it has a truthmaker. The statement that it has a truthmaker is itself a positive existential. In fact, it is the very same positive existential. The proposition that there is a cat is true just because there is a cat. What sort of explanation is that?—No explanation at all, and none the worse for that. (2001: 611–12)

When it comes to explaining truth, according to Lewis, what Truthmaker says about *that there is a cat* is on a par with what global TSB says about *that unicorns do not exist*.

But Lewis is wrong. Truthmaker says that each cat is a bit of being that makes *that there is a cat* true. In this way, each cat explains the truth of *that there is a cat*. This is significantly more than what global TSB says about *that unicorns do not exist*. For global TSB does not offer any bit of being to explain that truth. Global TSB offers only the triviality that worlds like ours in what exists are like ours in that *that unicorns do not exist* is true in them.[12]

So I object to Lewis's reply to Martin. But there is a deeper point here than merely an objection to that reply. That deeper point is that global TSB does not accommodate Truthmaker's principal motivation. For global TSB allows that literally nothing—no object, no property—necessitates or grounds the truth of negative existentials. This implies that global TSB fails to accommodate the idea or insight or intuition that truth—all truth—depends substantively on being.[13]

Cheaters fail to respect truth's dependence on being. Thus we can further demonstrate that global TSB does not accommodate the idea that all truth depends non-trivially on being

[12] Global TSB's claims about *positive* existentials are likewise trivial. For example, it is trivial that worlds alike with respect to what exists (and what properties which things have) are alike with respect to the truth of *that a cat exists*. But *that a cat exists* is true because a cat exists. And this, even with no help from global TSB, yields a bit of being—the cat—for that truth to depend on. Nothing analogous holds in the case of negative existentials. For example, *that unicorns do not exist* is true because unicorns do not exist; but this does not yield a bit of being for the truth of *that unicorns do not exist* to depend on.

[13] Consider the view that 'truth is supervenient on being' as understood by Bigelow: 'If something is true, then it would not be possible for it to be false unless either certain things were to exist which don't, or else certain things had not existed which do' (1988: 133). Taken as an attempted articulation of truth's substantive dependence on being, Bigelow's account has the same problems with negative existentials as does global TSB. Moreover, Bigelow's account has Truthmaker's problem that a claim like *that Fido is brown* turns out to depend on what exists (or fails to exist), as opposed to how things are.

by showing that global TSB is not able to catch cheaters. This further demonstration begins by considering the charge that 'counterfactuals of freedom' are ungrounded. Some philosophers say that God knows truths—and therefore that there are truths—of the following sort:

(1) If Curley had been offered a $35,000 bribe, he would have freely taken it.

As we shall see in Chapter 7, many object that nothing could make these alleged truths true. Suppose that one responded to this objection by saying that (1) is true just because Curley would have taken the bribe. (This mimics Lewis's remark in the passage quoted above that *that there are no unicorns* is true just because there are no unicorns.) This is, in fact, what I take Alvin Plantinga (1985: 374) to say about (1): 'For what grounds the truth of the counterfactual, we may say, is just that in fact Curley is such that if he had been offered a $35,000 bribe, he would have freely taken it.' I read Plantinga as asserting but a triviality: if (1) is true, then it is true because Curley would have freely accepted the $35,000 bribe, had it been offered to him.[14] Plantinga could even embellish his answer by adding that worlds alike with respect to what Curley and others would freely do in various situations are alike with respect to truths about what Curley and others would freely do in various situations.

Plantinga's answer isn't much of an answer, as Plantinga himself says (1985: 374). Even a cheater could offer that answer. TSB is supposed to catch cheaters. So TSB should have the resources to object to the sort of 'grounding' that even a

---

[14] I read Plantinga as denying that a truth must substantively depend on being, not as offering a substantive Suarezian supervenience base of the sort discussed in Ch. 2 (§IV) and 7 (§I). My reading is supported by Plantinga's remark, found on the same page as the comment quoted above: 'It seems to me much clearer that at least some counterfactuals of freedom are possibly true than that the truth of propositions must, in general, be grounded' (1985: 374).

cheater could offer. But global TSB does not. This is because, with respect to dependence on being, what global TSB says about negative existentials is exactly like what our embellished Plantinga says about counterfactuals of freedom. So any global TSBer who objects to Plantinga here invokes an unprincipled double standard.

Global TSBers might reply that a negative existential *denies* the existence of something. So there does not seem to *be* something (or some way things *are*) that a negative existential is about. Thus, they might argue, global TSB rightly releases negative existentials from the requirement that existing things (or those things being a certain way) ground their truth—while rightly refusing to release any other truths. Thus, they conclude, global TSB's treating negative existentials differently from the rest is principled, and exactly what we should expect from the correct account of truth's dependence on being.

This argument is just special pleading. But for special pleading, the reasoning behind this argument would release counterfactuals of freedom from the demand for grounding in what there is and how it is. For *counter*factuals of freedom are not about any *actual* action (or feature) of an entity. So there does not seem to *be* something (or some way things *are*) that a counterfactual is about. Thus, this reasoning suggests, global TSB should release counterfactuals of freedom from the requirement that existing things (or those things being a certain way) ground their truth.

We have seen that global TSB fails to say anything non-trivial about the truth of negative existentials. And we have seen that this failure reveals global TSB to be unfit not only to articulate the idea that truth depends substantively on being, but also to catch cheaters. But given the topics addressed in this book, the whole point of TSB is to articulate that idea and to catch cheaters. So TSBers should set global TSB aside.

Worldwide local TSB implies that, for each true negative existential, the having of some properties by some existing entities absolutely guarantees the truth of that negative existential. Presumably the relevant properties will include some sort of 'nothing more' property had by something like the universe (see Ch. 3). But however the details are worked out, worldwide local TSB implies that the truth of negative existentials depends substantively on being. Thus worldwide local TSB better articulates the idea that truth depends substantively on being, and better catches cheaters, than does global TSB. So TSBers should set global TSB aside and turn, instead, to worldwide local TSB.

V. Global Supervenience is not Dependence on Being

Assume that possible worlds are maximal abstract propositions, and that a world's *being actual* is nothing other than its *being true*.[15] For all p, p is 'true in' a possible world w just in case, necessarily, if w is actual (i.e., true), then p is true. So, to be true in all possible worlds with a certain feature F just is to be true if any world with that feature were true. Therefore, for p to be true in every F-world just is for p to be entailed by each of those F-worlds.

Let the F-worlds be those worlds like the actual world with respect to what exists and which things have which properties. That is, no matter which F-world were actual (true), all and only the things that actually exist would exist, and each of those things would exemplify all and only the properties it actually exemplifies. Then the claim that each and every truth globally supervenes on what things exist and which properties each of those things exemplifies is just another way of saying the

---

[15] If presentism is true, possible worlds are maximal only with respect to propositions that never change their truth-value. For ease of exposition, I run the argument to follow with worlds defined in terms of maximality *simpliciter*. But it is easy to see that the argument works just as well with a presentist-friendly account of possible worlds.

following: Each truth is entailed by every proposition that is an *F*-world.[16] Global TSB is a claim about entailment.

Global TSB is a claim about which abstract propositions entail each and every truth. This shows that global TSB does not articulate the idea that truth depends on being. For the idea that every truth *depends on being* is not the idea that every truth *is entailed by propositions of a certain sort*. Again, global TSB is not the right sort of claim to articulate the idea that truth depends on what there is and what it is like. So global TSB is of no interest to us. For the whole point of turning to TSB in this book was to find a thesis that articulates and accommodates the idea that truth depends on being but avoids Truthmaker's worst consequences.

This objection to global TSB does not require worlds to be propositions. It requires only that worlds be abstract representations of some sort or other. For the idea that each truth depends on being is not the idea that each truth is entailed by—or 'included in' or somehow itself 'represented by'—an abstract representation of some particular sort. Those who look to the ontology of possible worlds as a way to sidestep this objection must abandon the idea that worlds are abstract representations altogether. They must, instead, follow Lewis and say that possible worlds are universes like our own.

Even given the arguments of this section, global TSB might be importantly tied to truth's dependence on being. For suppose that presentism is false. Then a truth satisfies global TSB if that truth locally supervenes on all the objects that exist and all the properties that each of those objects has. Thus it is arguable that global TSB—the claim that each truth is entailed by every *F*-world—is a *direct result* of truth's dependence on being.[17] But even if global TSB is a result of that dependence, we ought

[16] If no two possible worlds can be exactly alike with respect to what is 'true in them', then global TSB implies that there is only one *F*-world.

[17] If presentism is correct, then there are truths that depend substantively on being—even truths that have truthmakers—but that violate global TSB (§III).

to move beyond global TSB and articulate that dependence itself. For it is the dependence of truth on being, rather than one of its sundry results, that TSB was supposed to articulate.

Truth's dependence on being arguably results in global TSB. In defending this, I glossed that dependence as each and every truth's locally supervening on all the objects that exist and all the properties that each of those objects has. This gloss is nothing other than worldwide local TSB. So, if we want the dependence of truth on being to lead to global TSB, then worldwide local TSB is how we should take that dependence. Thus we have our third reason that the TSBer should take worldwide local TSB, rather than global TSB, to articulate truth's dependence on being.

VI. Mere Supervenience is not Substantive Dependence

Every necessary truth is true in all possible worlds; so every necessary truth trivially satisfies *global* TSB. No matter what objects exist or which properties they exemplify, those objects having those properties will necessitate every necessary truth; so every necessary truth trivially satisfies *worldwide local* TSB.

Every necessary truth trivially satisfies both versions of TSB. So the claim that a necessary truth satisfies one or the other of these versions of TSB casts no light on how that truth non-trivially depends on being. Thus both versions of TSB fall short of articulating the way in which truth—all truth—is supposed to depend substantively on being. So, if either version of TSB is to articulate that dependence, it must be transformed into more than a thesis of mere (global or local) supervenience.[18]

So, if presentism is correct, I do not think that there is any interesting connection between truth's dependence on being and global TSB.

[18] TSBers might reply by restricting the claim that truth non-trivially depends on being. They might restrict this to contingent truths only. And they might add that TSB articulates that dependence (see Lewis 2001: 614). But recall that

This should remind us of Chapter 2's point that Truthmaker must say that there is more than to *making true* than mere necessitation, a point defended partly by way of necessary truths. And recall that Chapter 2 also defended that point by way of four arguments that had nothing to do with necessary truths. Each of those four arguments is easily adapted to further demonstrate that TSB, if it aims to articulate the idea that truth depends on being, must say more than that truth supervenes on being. Let me illustrate this by adapting just one of those arguments. (Nearly all of the arguments of this section, which are somewhat condensed, rely on claims defended in more detail in Ch. 2.)

Suppose that you endorse the following:

(2) If Queen Elizabeth II had been born in seventeenth-century Japan, she would have been a samurai warrior.

Suppose further that, as a natural result of endorsing (2), you believe that (2) (exists and) has the property of *being true*. And so you say that worlds like ours with respect to which things exist (including (2) itself) and the properties those things have (including *being true*) are worlds in which (2) is true. So (2)'s truth satisfies global TSB. Moreover, you say that, necessarily, given all the things that actually exist (including (2) itself) and all the properties those things actually have (including *being true*), (2) is true. So (2)'s truth satisfies worldwide local TSB.

We have just seen how a defender of (2) can accommodate either form of TSB, as currently formulated. But surely none of this accommodates what those who insist that all truth depends on being have in mind. This shows again that TSB—taken merely as a thesis of global or local supervenience—fails to articulate truth's dependence on being.

Ch. 2 (§II) argued that Truthmaker should not be restricted to contingent truths alone. And the first three arguments from that chapter are easily adapted to show that TSB—if it is meant to articulate truth's dependence on being and to catch cheaters—should not be thus restricted either.

We can make this same point in yet another way, a way that does not simply adapt an argument from Chapter 2. Consider:

(3) There is at least one electron.

In articulating how (3)'s truth depends on being, global TSB says *only* the following. Since (3) is true in our world, (3) is true in all worlds like ours with respect what exists and which properties those existents exemplify. So, in articulating how (3)'s truth depends on being, global TSB implies *nothing at all* about worlds that are not like ours with respect to all that exists or all the properties those existing things exemplify.

Similarly, given the truth of (3), worldwide local TSB says only that, necessarily, given all that exists, and all the properties those things have, (3) is true. Worldwide local TSB implies *nothing at all* about worlds that fail to be like ours by lacking some of the objects that actually exist; worldwide local TSB is likewise silent with respect to worlds in which some object fails to exemplify a property that it actually exemplifies.

In light of the points just made, we can see that, with respect to the dependence of (3)'s truth on being, both global and worldwide local TSB imply nothing at all about a world exactly like ours except that it contains one fewer marble in Australia. Since both versions of TSB say nothing at all about such a world, neither version tells us that (3)—which says that there is at least one electron—must be true in such a world.

I am not saying that either version of TSB tells us that, possibly, (3) is false in such a world. They do not have that absurd implication. On the contrary, and to repeat, global and worldwide local TSB have no implications at all regarding such a world. And because they have no such implications, they fail to tell us that the lack of a single antipodean marble cannot make all the difference with respect to the truth of (3), not even given what (3) asserts. But, given what (3) asserts, a full account of what (3)'s truth depends on would tell us this. So neither global nor worldwide local TSB is a full account of how (3)'s truth depends on being.

If either form of TSB hopes to articulate the idea that all truth depends on being, it must tell us what the dependence in question amounts to. So I think that it should add that, for each actual truth, what that truth is *about* is among the existing things and exemplified properties, in just the same sense of 'about' in which each truth must be about its truthmaker (Ch. 2, §§II–III). Moreover, it must say that a truth depends on what it is about.

With this in mind, consider once again:

(2) If Queen Elizabeth II had been born in seventeenth-century Japan, she would have been a samurai warrior.

Our recast global TSB is no longer satisfied by (2)'s being true in all worlds that include, among other things, (2)'s having the property of *being true*. Nor is our recast local TSB satisfied by the truth of (2)'s being necessitated by (2)'s having the property of *being true*. For both forms of TSB now insist that (2) is true only if there is that which (2) is appropriately about. And (2) is not thus about itself and its being true.

(3) is the claim that there is at least one electron. Our recast versions of TSB imply that if (3) is true, then (3)'s truth depends on those things that (3) is about. And so our recast versions of TSB have implications not just for worlds like ours in all that exists and all the properties those things exemplify, but also for worlds like ours merely with respect to the existence of whatever (3) is about. All those worlds, so TSB now implies, are worlds in which (3) is true.[19] Given that (3) is about each electron, we can conclude that worlds like ours but for a single Aussie marble are worlds in which (3) is true.

[19] This assumes that the relevant sort of *aboutness* involves necessitation (see Ch. 2, §III).

A defender of TSB also has to say that there is something, or some properties exemplified, that each necessary truth is about. She will have to say this, for example, with respect to Fermat's Last Theorem. I am not sure how this is supposed to go. So I shall not pursue this, beyond emphasizing the obvious point that anyone who thinks that all truth is substantively grounded in being must agree that each necessary truth is substantively grounded in being. A TSBer must agree, therefore, that there are some objects or properties (or the having of properties by objects) that Fermat's Last Theorem is appropriately about.

Since TSB is intended to articulate the idea that truth depends on being, let us now take both versions of TSB to say that each truth is about something, that is, about the existence of some objects or some properties had by some objects. Thus revised, TSB accommodates, and can be motivated by, an idea that Lewis relies on to motivate TSB. This is the idea that truths are about 'things' (Lewis 1999a: 206) and that 'every proposition, no matter what lesser subject matter it may have, is entirely about being' (Lewis 2003: 26). On the other hand, the original versions of TSB—both global and local—did not imply that each truth is about something. So those versions did not accommodate, and were not motivated by, the idea that truths are about things or about being.

This section has argued that TSB articulates truth's dependence on being only if it implies that each truth is appropriately about something and, moreover, for each truth, there are those entities and the having of properties by entities that that truth is thus about. So we are taking global TSB to imply this. Global TSB implies that each truth is about objects and properties, and that there are the objects and the properties that that truth is about. I think that, in general, that which a truth is about—in the relevant sense of 'about' (see Ch. 2, §III)—is sufficient for that truth. Given this, our revised global TSB implies that there is a local supervenience base for each truth, a base constituted by the entities, along with the having of properties by those entities, that that truth is about.

So global TSB, once it is revised in the way suggested in this section, implies that there is a local supervenience base for each truth. But if there is a local supervenience base of any sort for a truth, there is also a worldwide local supervenience base for that truth. Thus our revised global TSB implies that there is a worldwide local supervenience base for each truth—and so is committed to worldwide local TSB. This is the fourth reason that the TSBer, who aims to articulate and defend truth's dependence on being, should endorse worldwide local TSB.

We have seen that TSB, to articulate truth's dependence on being, must say that each truth locally supervenes on all that exists and all the properties those existents exemplify, and, moreover, that that local supervenience base includes what each truth is about. So let us now take TSB to say all of this. Finally, since TSB is supposed to catch cheaters, let us also take TSB to say that each and every truth has a local supervenience base that not only includes what that truth is about, but that is also free of *suspicious properties* (see Ch. 2, §IV).

The above four sections have argued, in four different ways, that the original version of TSB in terms of global supervenience alone fails to articulate the idea that truth depends substantively on being. Those sections have also argued that a revised version of TSB—TSB as we are now understanding it—does articulate the idea that all truth depends substantively on being. And I think we should all agree that TSB does articulate that idea. We should all agree on this, that is, except perhaps for truthmaker theorists. Truthmaker theorists might object that TSB, even as we are now understanding it, is too weak to capture the idea that truth depends on being. But even conceding this for the sake of argument, everyone should grant that if truth depends (in a substantive way) on being, then either Truthmaker or TSB is correct. This implies that if both

Truthmaker and TSB are false, then there are some truths that do not depend on being.

VII. TSB's Advantages Reconsidered

Advantage 1

Even given its new worldwide local supervenience form, supplemented with claims regarding aboutness and non-suspicious properties, TSB is still distinct from Truthmaker. Proof: TSB retains its first advantage. Truthmaker says that, for each and every truth, there is something or other whose mere existence necessitates that truth. Suppose, for example, that *that Fido is brown* is true. Then Truthmaker insists on something like the state of affairs of *Fido's being brown*, which state must have both Fido and *being brown* as essential constituents.

TSB insists on nothing like this. When it comes to the truth of *that Fido is brown*, TSB requires no more than a brown Fido. For given only a brown Fido, the truth of *that Fido is brown* locally supervenes on the entities that exist and all the non-suspicious properties that each of those entities has. Moreover, that truth's worldwide local supervenience base then includes what that truth is about, which is a brown Fido.

Advantage 2

Truthmaker requires that each true negative existential is in some way about, and is necessitated by, the positive existence of something. But that seems wrong. Moreover, even the best account of the truthmaker for a negative existential is subject to serious objections.

When it was taken as a thesis of mere global supervenience, TSB had none of Truthmaker's awkward commitments regarding negative existentials. But this is because global TSB has no (non-trivial) commitments at all regarding negative existentials, not even the commitment that true negative existentials depend (non-trivially) on being.

TSB, recast as a thesis of worldwide local supervenience, says something substantive about negative existentials. TSB says that a true negative existential is necessitated by, and is about, the positive existence of some entity (or entities) and the having of some non-suspicious property (or properties). But this is no more plausible than Truthmaker's claim that a true negative existential is necessitated by, and is about, the positive existence of some entity.

Moreover, I think that the best (least bad) account of the TSB-satisfying supervenience base for negative existential truths will be subject to nearly all of the objections faced by the best (least bad) account of the truthmaker for those truths. For the best account of that TSB-satisfying supervenience base will presumably involve something along the lines of a 'nothing more' or 'totality' property.[20]

TSB has no advantage, with respect to negative existential truths, over Truthmaker. So, just as they gave us a reason to doubt Truthmaker, negative existential truths give us a reason to doubt TSB.

Advantage 3

World W_1 includes X. It seems that there should be another world that differs from W_1 only in that that world does not include X (and X's parts, etc.). Truthmaker rules out such a world, which is to its discredit. But so does our recast TSB. For let W_2 be a world in which X does not exist. So, in W_2, it is true that X does not exist. According to TSB, something exists

---

[20] Ch. 3 (§IV) pointed out five problems with Truthmaker's relying on a totality state to make negative existentials true. The first four of those can easily be transformed into problems with TSB's thus relying on a 'nothing more' or 'totality' property.

or something has a property in W_2, the existence or having of which necessitates *that* X *does not exist*. That something cannot exist in W_1, and that property cannot be thus exemplified in W_1, because *that* X *does not exist* is false in W_1. Thus, given TSB, it cannot be that the *only* difference between W_1 and W_2 is that X (and X's parts, etc.) exists in one but not in the other.

According to TSB, we can remove X only by replacing it with either a new object or a new exemplification of a property.[21] The claim that removing an entity results in (for example) the exemplification of a new property is no better than the claim that removing an entity results in (for example) the existence of a new state of affairs. So TSB forfeits its third advantage over Truthmaker.[22]

VIII. TSB and Truthmaker

TSB says that every truth is necessitated by, and is about, the positive existence of this or that entity or the positive

[21] This result of TSB would not be bad if, e.g., removing X meant only additions along the lines of *being true* coming to be exemplified by *that* X *does not exist*. But we have already seen that, lest it be unfit to catch cheaters, TSB cannot let propositions and their truth-values carry the supervenience load (§VI). So, given TSB, removing X must result in additions besides exemplifications of *being true*. Besides, if the TSBer insisted that removing X meant only adding *being true* to an otherwise false proposition, TSB would still lose its third advantage over Truthmaker. For the Truthmaker theorist could then follow suit and say that removing X requires only adding the state of affairs of *that* X *does not exist's being true*. (Of course, this move is no more adequate to Truthmaker's own demands than the analogous move is to those of TSB.)

[22] One other objection that Lewis raises to Truthmaker suggests a parallel objection to TSB. Lewis (2001: 611) points out that the truthmaker for *that nothing contingent exists* could not be a necessarily existing entity, lest *that nothing contingent exists* be a necessary truth. So its truthmaker would have to be contingent. Necessarily, no contingently existing truthmaker exists if it is true that nothing contingent exists. So Truthmaker implies that *that nothing contingent exists* is necessarily false, and this is a cost. TSB has a similar cost. TSB must say that the following is necessarily false: *that no contingent thing exists and no contingently exemplified properties are exemplified*.

exemplification of this or that (non-suspicious) property. TSB's vision of the world is thus very much like that of Truth-maker, which says that every truth is necessitated by, and is about, the positive existence of this or that (Ch. 3, §V). Truthmaker and TSB are variations on the same misguided theme.

TSB implies that every truth locally supervenes on which things exist and which properties each of those things has (and which relations those things stand in). Suppose that whenever a thing has a property, there is a corresponding state of affairs of that thing's having that property. For example, suppose that if x is F, there is the state of *x's being* F. (And suppose that if x stands in R to y, there is the state of *x's standing in* R *to* y.) Suppose also that every state of affairs has its constituents essentially. Then there is no substantial difference between Truthmaker and TSB. Then Truthmaker is correct if and only if TSB is correct.

I doubt that, for every object that has a property, there is a state of affairs of that object's having that property. And I see no reason to think that, if states of affairs do exist, they have their constituents essentially. So I think that Truthmaker and TSB differ. But the point here is that the differences between them, if any, come down to the question of the existence and essences of states of affairs. But for their implications regarding this single question, Truthmaker and TSB go hand in hand.

In much of what follows in this book, the difference—if any—between Truthmaker and TSB makes no difference. For example, consider the charge that presentists cheat when they affirm that the Trojans were conquered. Whether this charge comes in the form of TSB or Truthmaker makes no difference. For what is at issue is not whether there is a state of affairs of *the universe's having the property of being such that the Trojans were conquered* or, instead, whether the universe simply has this property. Rather, what is at issue is whether the truth of *that the Trojans were conquered*, given presentism, requires the world to have that property at all. Also at issue is whether that property is suspicious. Issues like these can be pursued independently of what, if anything, divides Truthmaker from TSB.

5

MODALITY

That Fido is possibly black is true. Suppose I said that its truth-maker is partly constituted by the irreducible modal property of *being possibly black*. Then some will call me a cheater. For they will object that irreducible modal properties are suspicious (see, e.g., Sider 2001: 40–1). But no defender of Truthmaker or TSB should thus object. For, as this chapter argues, Truthmaker and TSB imply that there is irreducible *de re* modality, which suggests that certain truths are made true, in part, by irreducible modal properties. The heart of this argument is the claim that Truthmaker and TSB are inconsistent with the leading reductions of *de re* modality, a claim defended by the bulk of this chapter. We shall also see that even those who reject Truthmaker and TSB should embrace irreducible *de re* modality.

I. Lewis's Reduction

According to David Lewis, our universe is the 'actual world'. The other possible worlds—one for every way things could be—are also *bona fide* universes, like ours in kind. Each of us exists entirely in the actual world. But we have 'counterparts' in many possible worlds.

According to Lewis, for any object O and property F, O's *being possibly* F is reduced to some of O's counterparts being

F; *O*'s *being essentially* F is reduced to all of *O*'s counterparts being *F*; *O*'s *being accidentally* F is reduced to *O*'s being *F* but some of *O*'s counterparts failing to be *F*. In this way, the inhabitants of other worlds generate Lewis's reduction of *de re* modal properties of actual objects. (See Lewis 1986.)

This brief summary of Lewis's reduction leaves a lot out. But it includes all that is required to make the main point of this section. For that point requires only that Lewis's reduction of this or that actual object's having this or that *de re* modal property typically involves entities in possible worlds other than the actual world.

Recall brown Fido. Fido is possibly black. Given Lewis's account of modality, Fido's being possibly black is reduced to the existence of black counterparts of Fido. Now consider:

(1) Fido is possibly black.

Given Lewis's reduction of what it is for Fido to be possibly black, (1) is made true by any and all of Fido's black counterparts. None of Fido's counterparts exists in the actual world. Thus (1) is actually true, but (1) has no actually existing truthmaker.[1] I shall argue that Truthmaker militates against this

---

[1] Perhaps Fido's being possibly black is reduced to a combination of the actual brown Fido and his other-worldly black counterparts. (After all, what makes them *counterparts* of Fido is partly a matter of the way Fido actually is.) Even so, that combination does not exist in the actual world in its entirety; so, according to Lewis, it does not actually exist (see Lewis 1986: 211). This is enough for the argument of this section.

Lewis (2003) would say that 'Fido *qua* possibly black' is an entity that actually exists and also makes it true that Fido is possibly black. But Lewis should not say this. For, as Lewis (2003) himself insists, Fido *qua* possibly black is identical with Fido. And, I add, it is a mistake for Lewis to say that Fido himself makes *that Fido is possibly black* true. This is because, according to Lewis, *that Fido is possibly black* is a relational claim, a claim about Fido and how he is related to certain other-worldly black things. Lewis's saying that Fido himself is a truthmaker for *that Fido is possibly black* is like my saying that John himself is a truthmaker for *that John is taller than Mary*. (And note that John's truthmaking powers are not enhanced if I name him 'John *qua* taller than Mary'.)

result and, more generally, against there being any actual truth without an actual truthmaker.

That a horse exists is actually true. *That a unicorn exists* is not actually true. But, given Lewis's account of modality, truthmakers for both of these claims exist: there are horses and there are (in other possible worlds) unicorns. So, given Lewis's account of modality, we cannot explain the difference in actual truth between these two claims simply by saying that truthmakers for one of these claims exist, but not for the other.

Yet we can give a Truthmaker-based explanation of why one of these claims is actually true and the other is not, an explanation consistent with Lewis's other-worldly unicorns. *That a horse exists* is actually true because it has an actually existing truthmaker. *That a unicorn exists* is not actually true because it fails to have an actually existing truthmaker.

Moreover, suppose that I were to claim that *that a unicorn exists* is actually true, even though it lacks an actual truthmaker. Then surely I cheat. Then I am not respecting the dependence of actual truth on actual being. I am cheating and failing to respect this dependence even if, like Lewis, I believe that merely possible unicorns really do exist.

So I conclude that a corollary of Truthmaker is that, in general, actual truths have actual truthmakers.[2] But Lewis cannot satisfy this corollary of Truthmaker when it comes to claims of *de re* modality. For, as we have seen, given Lewis's account of modality, *that Fido is possibly black* is actually true but lacks an actual truthmaker. So Lewis's story about what grounds truths of *de re* modality conflicts with Truthmaker.

---

[2] I say that everything exists in the actual world. So I think that if every truth has a truthmaker, then every actual truth has an actual truthmaker. Indeed, I think that this 'corollary' of Truthmaker just is Truthmaker itself. But Lewis does not. For Lewis thinks that some things do not exist in the actual world. Nevertheless, the point of the argument in the text above is that even truthmaker theorists with Lewis's views on actuality should say that actual truths must have actual truthmakers.

This is surprising. For many take Lewis's account of modality to be tailor-made to satisfy Truthmaker (see esp. Lewis 2003; see also Sider 2001: 41).

In light of the point just made, Lewis could reply that truthmaker theorists should deny that actual truths require actual truthmakers. But denying this is something truthmaker theorists should see as a cost. So Lewis's account of modality has costs when it comes to Truthmaker.[3] And that Lewis's account of modality has any such costs is surprising. For, to repeat, many take Lewis's account to be tailor-made for Truthmaker, as opposed to an account that Truthmaker can perhaps accommodate, but only by giving up its intuitively plausible corollary that actual truths have actual truthmakers.

The above arguments show that Lewis's story about what grounds modal claims has costs from the perspective of Truthmaker. The same reasoning shows, *mutatis mutandis*, that Lewis's story has costs with respect to TSB. For TSBers should demand that actual truths have an actual TSB-satisfying supervenience base. So Lewis's account of modality fails to deliver everything that a defender of Truthmaker and TSB could want.

I just blinked. But, possibly, I did not blink. Presumably, my not blinking is consistent with everything else having gone (pretty much) just as it actually did. So Lewis must say that, in some other universe, there is a planet that has been (pretty much) just like Earth in every way from the dawn of history until my recent blinking, though my counterpart on that

---

[3] This cost is just one of Lewis's problems with claims that are true in a world w but are about entities that exist in worlds other than w. The most extreme examples involve trans-world individuals, i.e., objects with proper parts in more than one world. Lewis (1986: 211) himself concedes that although such individuals really do exist, they are impossible. That is bad enough. Moreover, as Hudson (1997) points out, this concession implies that, for every trans-world individual O, *that* O *exists* is both true and also necessarily false.

planet does not blink. That planet is not ours, but it is peopled by beings like us in virtually every deed and thought. So exact duplicates of the entire Hollywood A-list and attendant hangers-on and paparazzi reside on that planet. Moreover, exact duplicates of the flora and fauna of the Amazon basin can be found there. And so on.

Understandably, most deny that there is such a planet. More generally, most deny that there is a Lewis-style possible world—a universe akin to our own—for every possibility. And anyone, including any truthmaker theorist or TSBer, who denies this must reject Lewis's reduction of modality. So, even if Truthmaker did not suggest that actual truths have actual truthmakers, and TSB that actual truths have an actual TSB-satisfying supervenience base, Lewis's reduction would still be unacceptable to virtually all truthmaker theorists and TSBers.

II. Abstract Worlds Reduction

Most deny that there is a Lewis-style possible world for every possibility. There is, however, significantly more support for 'abstract' possible worlds. Abstract worlds 'represent' possibilities. The actual world represents how things are, and the merely possible worlds represent how things could be. And, so the lore goes, an object is possibly a certain way if and only if a world represents it as being that way.

For example, I am possibly forty feet tall if and only if a possible world represents me as being forty feet tall. We could defend one direction of this biconditional as follows: I am possibly forty feet tall; because of this, some maximal abstracta representing me as forty feet tall are possibly actual; therefore a possible world represents me as being forty feet tall. Many abstract worlders reason in this way. That is, many begin with *de re* modality and go from there in giving an account of possible worlds (Plantinga 1974; Kripke 1980: 19 n. 18; van Inwagen 1986: 187).

But I shall ignore accounts of abstract possible worlds that presuppose *de re* modality. I am interested, instead, in those abstract worlders—such as Hazen (1979), Heller (1998), and Sider (2002)—who follow Lewis in reducing *de re* modality to possible worlds. These abstract worlders purport to reduce my being possibly forty feet tall to my being forty feet tall in some abstract possible world. Again, they would say that my being possibly forty feet tall just is my being represented as being forty feet tall by an abstract possible world.

I shall argue that defenders of Truthmaker and TSB should object to such a reduction. The first step in that argument involves something more simple-minded than a reduction of *de re* modality to abstract worlds. The first step considers the alleged reduction of my being possibly forty feet tall to the truth of this abstract proposition:

A: Possibly, Merricks is forty feet tall.

Reducing my being possibly forty feet tall to the truth of A violates the core intuition behind Truthmaker and TSB: truth depends on what there is and (for TSB) what it is like. Saying that the truth of a proposition is what it is for me to be possibly forty feet tall, and so is what my being that way depends on, turns this core intuition on its head.

This core intuition notwithstanding, Truthmaker and TSB should allow that my *being such that* p *is true* is reduced to—and so depends on—the truth of *p*. For I do not think this really violates Truthmaker's and TSB's ban on my being a certain way's depending on a proposition's truth. For my 'being such that *p* is true' is not really my being any way at all. It is, instead, simply my existing and—we are now done talking about me—*p*'s being true.[4]

---

[4] My being a parent is not a way that I am intrinsically, of course, but I do think that it is a way that I really am. On the other hand, consider my being such

Genuine *de re* modality is a matter of how objects really are. So I think that *de re* modality is not akin to *being such that* p *is true*. As we shall see, however, Hazen (1979), Heller (1998), and Sider (2002) may be thinking of *de re* modality as relevantly like *being such that* p *is true*. This view of *de re* modality is the topic of the next section. But let us ignore it for now.

Let us assume, for now, that *de re* modality is a matter of the way objects really are. As I shall argue in this section, given this assumption, truthmaker theorists and TSBers cannot be abstract world reductionists about *de re* modality. That argument begins, as we have seen, with the core intuition behind Truthmaker and TSB, the intuition that truth depends on what there is and what it is like, rather than the other way around.

We have seen that defenders of Truthmaker and TSB should deny that my being possibly forty feet tall is reduced to, and so depends on, the *truth* of any proposition, including:

A: Possibly, Merricks is forty feet tall.

Now consider an account that reduces my being possibly forty feet tall to the *possible truth* of a proposition. Specifically, consider an account that reduces my being that way to the following proposition's *being possibly true*:

B: Merricks is forty feet tall.[5]

that the Empire State Building is taller than the Washington Monument. Not only is this not a way that I am intrinsically, it is also not a way that I am at all. And the same goes for my being such that *p* is true. Again, it is simply my existing and—we are now done talking about me—*p*'s being true.

   [5] Let me note one hurdle that this reduction—and all the reductions to follow in this section—must get over. This reduction is partly motivated by the idea that all irreducible modal properties are suspicious. Thus motivated, this reduction had better not take B's being possibly true to amount to B's having the irreducible modal property of *being possibly true*. Moreover, lest we face an unseemly regress, B's *being possibly true* cannot be reduced to a possibly true proposition's representing B as true. In general, this sort of reduction must give a proposition's being possibly true special treatment; i.e., a proposition's being

This account resembles the proposed reduction of my being possibly forty feet tall to A's *being true*. Both say that some existing object is a certain way—namely, I myself am possibly forty feet tall—because of the relation of a proposition to truth.

Defenders of Truthmaker and TSB say that a proposition's being true depends on what there is and (for TSB) how it is. And, since the denial of any ungrounded falsehood would itself be an ungrounded truth, they had better add that a proposition's failing to be true (i.e., its being false) also so depends. More generally, I think that defenders of Truthmaker or TSB should say that a proposition's *relation to truth* depends on the way things are, rather than vice versa. As a result, they should deny that my being possibly forty feet tall is reduced to B's being possibly true.

Moreover, consider:

(2) The Trojans were conquered.

Suppose (2) is true. According to the presentist, the Trojans do not exist. Nor do any past events, such as the Trojans' long-ago defeat. Indeed, given presentism, there exists nothing that would obviously ground (2)'s truth. So both Truthmaker and TSB, when conjoined with (2)'s truth, threaten to rule out presentism.

Presentists might say that (2) is made true by the universe's being such that the Trojans were conquered. Moreover, they might add that the universe's being such that the Trojans were conquered just is—is reduced to, is nothing more than—the past truth of *that the universe is such that the Trojans are being*

possibly true cannot be treated as just another case of *de re* modality, with the proposition being the *res* and *possibly true* the modal property. (One example of 'special treatment' says that a proposition is possibly true just in case its denial is not analytic.) But this special treatment, whatever it turns out to be, must also deliver *de dicto* modality; so among its deliverances must be, e.g., some propositions that are possibly true; equivalently, it must deliver the result (by offering a reduction of this result) that some propositions stand in the *possibly exemplifying* relation to *being true*.

conquered. (A smart-alecky presentist might even proclaim that *being such that the Trojans were conquered* is relevantly like *being such that* p *is true*.)

These presentists purport to reduce the universe's being such that the Trojans were conquered to the universe's being represented as being a certain way by a proposition that *was true*. The modal reduction involving B purports to reduce my being possibly forty feet tall to my being represented as being a certain way by a proposition that *is possibly true*. The resemblance between these two reductions illustrates another reason that truthmaker theorists and TSBers should deny that my being possibly forty feet tall is reduced to B's being possibly true. They should deny this because failing to deny it compromises their ability to catch cheaters.

Defenders of Truthmaker and TSB ought to deny that my being a certain way is reduced to a proposition's relation to truth. In particular, they ought to deny that my being possibly forty feet tall is reduced to the possible truth of B. Note that B's 'non-maximality' is irrelevant to this objection. Even if B were a maximal proposition, the objection would stand.

With this in mind, let Γ be one of the maximal propositions that entail, among other things, that I am forty feet tall. The above reason to deny that my being possibly forty feet tall is reduced to the possible truth of B is also a reason to deny that it is reduced to the possible truth of Γ. And it is a reason to deny, more generally, that an object's being possibly a certain way is reduced to its being represented as being that way by a particular possibly true maximal proposition.[6]

---

[6] Note that Γ's entailing a *singular* proposition involving me is irrelevant to this objection. Suppose that we try to reduce my being possibly forty feet tall to the possible truth of Δ, which is a maximal proposition that entails, among other things, that someone or other *very much like me* is forty feet tall. Given Truthmaker and TSB, my being possibly forty feet tall should not depend on Δ's relation to truth any more than it should depend on Γ's.

Suppose that abstract worlds are maximal possibly true propositions.[7] Then Truthmaker and TSB provide a reason to deny that an object's being possibly a certain way is reduced to its being that way in a particular world. Of course, no abstract worlds reduction says that my being possibly forty feet tall is reduced to my being represented as being forty feet tall by Γ (and Γ's being possibly true). Rather, my being possibly forty feet tall is purportedly reduced to my being represented as being forty feet tall *by some possible world or other*. But this reduction commits the same sin as those above. It says that the way something is—my being possibly forty feet tall—depends on propositions and their relations to truth. This is in direct opposition to the core intuition behind Truthmaker and TSB, which is that propositions' relations to truth depend on the way things are, not the other way around.

I have just argued that if abstract possible worlds are propositions, then Truthmaker and TSB undermine reductions of *de re* modality to abstract possible worlds. But it is controversial whether worlds are propositions. So, one might conclude, the above reasoning does not touch abstract worlds reductions as such.

That conclusion is too hasty. This is partly because taking abstract worlds to be propositions is not as controversial as it might at first appear. For example, one apparent rival to worlds as propositions is the thesis that abstract worlds are sets of ordered pairs of, first, ordered quadruples of numbers and, second, numbers (Heller 1998). But the thesis that worlds are such sets does not deny that worlds are propositions. Indeed, this thesis goes hand in hand with a reduction of propositions to such sets (see Quine 1969). Thus this thesis goes hand in hand with the claim that possible worlds are propositions.

---

[7] Or suppose that they are possibly true propositions that are maximal with respect to propositions that never change their truth-value (see Ch. 4, §III).

Alvin Plantinga explicitly distinguishes abstract 'states of affairs', which can 'obtain', from propositions, which can be true.[8] But even as he makes this distinction, Plantinga concedes that perhaps abstract states of affairs are one and the same as abstract propositions (Plantinga 1974: 45; see also Plantinga 1987: 192). Presumably, he concedes this because of the striking parallels between abstract states of affairs and propositions and between *obtaining* and *being true*. The parallels are so striking that, in my opinion, we should unequivocally insist that Plantinga's abstract states of affairs are propositions. Again, what initially seemed to be a competitor to identifying worlds with propositions goes hand in hand with that identification.

Robert Adams (1974) denies that a possible world is a proposition. He says, instead, that a possible world is a set of propositions. According to Adams, for me to be represented as being forty feet tall by a world is for that world to have *that Merricks is forty feet tall* as a member. That set is a *possible* world only because, among other things, that member is *possibly true*. Thus a reduction of *de re* modality invoking Adams-style worlds reduces my being possibly forty feet tall to, among other things, the possible truth of *that Merricks is forty feet tall*. Obviously enough, the above Truthmaker- and TSB-based objections to reducing *de re* modality to the possible truth of propositions have purchase here.

Moreover, as we shall see, those objections even have purchase on abstract worlders who (like, e.g., Hazen (1979)) say nothing about the nature of possible worlds other than that these worlds are not the 'concrete' worlds of Lewis's multiverse. This is because, whatever else they may be, abstract worlds are abstract representations of some sort. And the

---

[8] Plantinga's abstract states of affairs are not to be confused with the states of affairs—the events, the Russellian facts—that have played a prominent role throughout this book.

abstract representation that is the actual world, unlike the abstract representations that are the merely possible worlds, is *accurate*.

Perhaps a representation's *being accurate* is nothing other than its *being true*. Then all abstract representations are presumably abstract propositions, and we are right back to worlds as propositions. So suppose, just for the sake of argument, that an abstract representation's *being accurate* need not be the same as its *being true*. Nevertheless, *being true* is a species of *being accurate*: a true proposition is an accurate representation.

Now consider a reduction of my being possibly forty feet tall to the *accuracy* of an abstractum A*, which represents me as being possibly forty feet tall. Neither the truthmaker theorist nor the TSBer should accept this reduction. Both should deny that my being possibly forty feet tall is reduced to, and so depends on, the accuracy of this abstract representation.

They should deny this because their insistence that truth depends on being commits them to the more general claim that the accuracy of an abstract representation depends on being. After all, suppose that an abstract representation's relation to accuracy in general did not depend on being. Then I think that there would be no reason to expect such dependence in the case of an abstract proposition's relation to truth, since truth is a species of accuracy. Truthmaker and TSB, in insisting on such dependence only in the case of truth, would be guilty of special pleading.

Truthmaker theorists and TSBers alike must deny that my being possibly forty feet tall is reduced to representation A*'s being accurate. They should say, instead, that if A* is an accurate representation, this is because I am possibly forty feet tall. And, in light of the above arguments involving worlds as propositions, truthmaker theorists and TSBers ought to go further. They ought to deny that my being possibly forty feet tall depends on how abstract representations are related to *being accurate*. As a result, they should reject all abstract worlds reductions of *de re* modality.

Truthmaker theorists and TSBers should reject all abstract worlds reductions of modality. That is the main point of this section. But there is a second point. It is that everyone—even those who deny Truthmaker and TSB—should reject all abstract worlds reductions of modality.

My defence of this second point begins by noting that Truthmaker and TSB are both false if and only if there are truths without truthmakers and truths without a TSB-satisfying supervenience base. Suppose that we think there are such truths, and therefore that we deny Truthmaker and TSB. Perhaps, for example, we think that one such truth is *that hobbits do not exist*.

So we deny that the truth of *that hobbits do not exist* depends on being in the substantive ways articulated by Truthmaker and TSB. But we should still say that its truth depends on being in a trivial way. That is, we should still say that *that hobbits do not exist* is true *because* hobbits do not exist. (Everyone should say this.) More to the point, we should still object that it gets things backwards to say that hobbits do not exist *because* of the truth of *that hobbits do not exist*.

The point here is general. Even if we reject Truthmaker and TSB, we should agree with one thing that Truthmaker and TSB say. We should agree that the way you and I and other non-propositions are does not depend on propositions' being true or, more generally, on how representations are related to accuracy.

As a result, even if we reject Truthmaker and TSB, we should deny that I am possibly forty feet tall because A—which says that, possibly, Merricks is forty feet tall—is true. More generally, we should deny that my being possibly forty feet tall depends on a representation's relation to *being accurate*. More generally still, we should endorse the above Truthmaker- and

TSB-inspired argument against abstract worlds reductions of *de re* modality. [9]

III. Broadly Quinean Reduction

Take any true proposition *p*. I am such that *p* is true. Plausibly, my being such that *p* is true is nothing other than my existing and *p*'s being true. So my being such that *p* is true is reduced, in part, to *p*'s being true. Thus my being such that *p* is true depends on *p*'s being true. So my being such that *p* is true depends on a proposition's relation to truth. If *de re* modal properties were relevantly like *being such that* p *is true*—and if *de re* modal properties' being that way were consistent with Truthmaker and TSB—then the argument of the preceding section would be in trouble.

With this in mind, consider an account of modality that says that all *de re* modality (if there is *de re* modality at all) is relative to a feature or property. That is, this account allows for cases of *de re* modality only along the lines of *x*'s, *qua F*, being necessarily *G*. Moreover, this account reduces this to, first, *x*'s being *F*, and second, the necessary truth of the proposition *that all Fs are Gs*. Given this account, *being*, qua F, *necessarily* G is relevantly like *being such that* p *is true*. For, according to this account, *being*, qua F, *necessarily* G is, at least in part, nothing more than a proposition's relation to truth.

Quine (1960: 195–200) would take this account to be devoid of *de re* modality. I think he is right. For, as I noted in the last section, *de re* modality is a matter of the (modal) ways objects are. On this account, however, an object's 'modal properties'

---

[9] Lewis (1986: 136–91) and I (Merricks 2003*a*) raise further objections to reducing modal properties to how objects are represented by abstract worlds.

are no more a matter of the ways that object is than my 'being such that *p* is true' is a matter of the ways that I am. And if this account really does eliminate *de re* modality, then it is inconsistent with Truthmaker, which has *de re* modality at its core (Ch. 1, §III). It is likewise inconsistent with TSB, which requires objects and properties to necessitate the truth of claims.

But counterpart-theoretic abstract world reductionists, such as Hazen (1979), Heller (1998), and Sider (2002), would resist my (and Quine's) view of this Quinean account of modality. They would take this account of modality to reduce, rather than eliminate, *de re* modality. Suppose they are right. Truthmaker and TSB can still be shown to be inconsistent with this Quinean account. So, even if we concede that this account reduces, rather than eliminates, *de re* modality, we can still show that it fails to reconcile Truthmaker and TSB to a reduction of *de re* modality in terms of how propositions (or abstract representations) are related to truth (or accuracy).

It is easy to see why this broadly Quinean reduction of *de re* modality is inconsistent with Truthmaker. Truthmaker says that, for each truth, there is something that, *by its mere existence*, makes that truth true. This implies that, for each truth, there is something that, *qua* existing, necessitates that truth (Ch. 1, §§II–III). But this implication rules out Quinean reductionism. After all, the claim that *x*, *qua* existing, is necessarily such that *p* is true is equivalent to the un-Quinean claim that *x* is essentially such that *p* is true.[10]

---

[10]   Perhaps the Quinean can say that, if *p* is a necessary truth, then *x*, *qua* existing, necessitates *p*. And they might say the same if *p* is *that something exists*. But, given the Quinean reduction, no other truths can be necessitated by something *qua* existing.

Lewis (1986) takes the counterpart relation to be sortal-relative. So Lewis, no less than Quine, denies that objects, *qua* existing, are necessarily a certain way. So Lewis, no less than Quine, denies that objects, *qua* existing, necessitate truths. This is another reason that Lewis (1986) cannot satisfy Truthmaker, a reason in addition to those advanced in § I.

Unlike Truthmaker, TSB does not imply that for each truth, there is something that, *qua* existing, necessitates that truth. Nevertheless, like Truthmaker, TSB cannot be reconciled to this broadly Quinean reduction of *de re* modality. The argument for this begins by pointing out that, according to TSB, every truth has a local supervenience base. So TSB says that every truth is *necessitated by* what exists and which properties those existing things have.

Quinean reductionists cannot allow this necessitation to go unreduced. So, if they want to accommodate TSB, they must reduce the necessitation of the truth of a claim by objects and properties. Here is how their reduction will go. First, there are objects that have properties. Second, it is a *necessary truth* that, given that those objects have those properties, that claim is true.

Quineans require many, and varied, necessary truths to accommodate TSB. Consider what they require to accommodate TSB with respect to, for example, the truth of *that one ought not to spread butter with one's fish knife*. TSB implies that this truth is necessitated by the exemplification of (non-suspicious) properties and the existence of objects. The Quinean reduction of this necessitation requires there to be a necessary truth to the effect that, given those objects and their having those properties, then *that one ought not to spread butter with one's fish knife* is true.

I think that there is a necessary truth to this effect. But I think that there is that necessary truth *because* the truth of *that one ought not to spread butter with one's fish knife* is necessitated by (supervenes on) the relevant objects and properties. Our Quinean reductionists cannot say anything like this, since they must say that this necessitation (supervenience) is partly reduced to the relevant necessary truth. These Quineans must say this necessitation holds *because*, at least in part, there already is that necessary truth. But this claim is not plausible. So the Quineans' way of accommodating TSB is not plausible. Moreover, the necessary truth that the Quinean account requires—a necessary truth that presumably mentions (e.g.) quarks in the antecedent, and has a claim of etiquette for a consequent, so is not remotely analytic—should not be any more acceptable to these Quineans than the unreduced necessary connections they so steadfastly oppose.

There is another problem with the Quinean attempt to accommodate TSB. Suppose that O is the only object. Let $F_1 \ldots F_n$ be all its properties. Let p be a truth. TSB implies that p is necessitated by (O's existence and by) O's having $F_1 \ldots F_n$. The Quinean must reduce this necessitation to, first, O's having $F_1 \ldots F_n$ and, second, its being necessarily true *that if something has* $F_1 \ldots F_n$, *then* p *is true.*

But if we stop here—if this really is all there is to the 'necessitation' of p by O's having $F_1 \ldots F_n$—then we fail to accommodate TSB. For this kind of 'necessitation' does not, all by itself, deliver a local supervenience base for p. We get that base only if we can add that the antecedent of the necessarily true conditional, which is *that something has* $F_1 \ldots F_n$, is true. For only then can this reduction guarantee that p is true. And p must be true if it has a local supervenience base.

So suppose that *that something has* $F_1 \ldots F_n$ is true. Defenders of TSB will insist that this truth depends on being. They will insist that this truth is made true by—so is necessitated by—O's having $F_1 \ldots F_n$. So O's having $F_1 \ldots F_n$ necessitates *that something has* $F_1 \ldots F_n$. But Quineans cannot let this necessitation of a truth by objects and properties go unreduced. Quineans must reduce this necessitation to O's having $F_1 \ldots F_n$ and its being necessarily true *that if something has* $F_1 \ldots F_n$, *then it is true that something has* $F_1 \ldots F_n$. But, much as before, this gets us the truth of *that something has* $F_1 \ldots F_n$ only if its antecedent is true. Presumably, its antecedent is necessitated by O's having $F_1 \ldots F_n$.

This last bit of necessitation could be reduced in broadly Quinean style by repeating the step just made. A regress (or circle) looms. By the lights of TSB, this regress (or circle) is vicious, since it is a regress (or circle) of grounding. Moreover, at each step, part of what grounds *that something has* $F_1 \ldots F_n$ is the necessary truth of the conditional *that if something has* $F_1 \ldots F_n$, *then it is true that something has* $F_1 \ldots F_n$. But surely this is contrary to the spirit of TSB. Surely at least some truths are entirely 'about things'. At least some truths are grounded entirely by objects that exist and their properties. But combining a broadly Quinean reduction of *de re* modality with TSB implies that every truth is grounded, in part, by the necessary truth of a conditional proposition.

When it comes to Truthmaker and TSB, abstract world reductionists face a dilemma. One horn is that their view, in terms of the locus of modality, is relevantly like the broadly Quinean approach. Then their view is that my being possibly forty feet tall is relevantly analogous to my being such that p is true—and so my being that way can plausibly be reduced to, at least in part, a proposition's relation to truth. But any such account of abstract worlds cannot deliver the sort of necessitation required by both Truthmaker and TSB. Some, and perhaps all, abstract worlds reductions of modality are impaled upon this first horn.

But perhaps some abstract world reductionists do not endorse a Quinean reduction (or elimination) of *de re* modality. They can deny that an object's having a modal property is akin to my being such that p is true. They would then avoid the first horn. But not the second. For given that denial, as we saw in §II, they cannot reconcile Truthmaker and TSB with the claim that an object's modal properties depend on how abstract representations are related to accuracy.

IV. Irreducible *de re* Modality

Truthmaker theorists and TSBers should say that *de re* modality cannot be reduced to Lewis-style possible worlds (§I) or to abstract possible worlds (§§II–III). More generally, Truthmaker and TSB undermine any attempt to reduce *de re* modality to how an object is *represented* (§§II-III). So, for example, they undermine attempts to reduce *de re* modality to what a fiction represents (as in Rosen 1990). So I conclude that Truthmaker and TSB imply that *de re* modality cannot be reduced at all.[11]

One might opt for rejecting *de re* modality altogether, rather than embracing irreducible *de re* modality. But this option forces one to reject Truthmaker and TSB. For each truthmaker is *essentially* such that its truth is true. And TSB says that, for all true propositions *p*, it is *impossible* that all actual objects exist and have the properties that they actually have and *p* be false. By being committed to a necessary connection between, on the one hand, objects and which properties they exemplify and, on the other, true claims, TSB is no less committed to *de re* modality than is Truthmaker.

Truthmaker and TSB lead to irreducible *de re* modality. A corollary of this is that Truthmaker and TSB are committed to irreducible *de re* modal properties. For suppose that *that Fido is possibly black* is true. Truthmaker demands that it have a truthmaker. TSB demands that it have a TSB-satisfying supervenience base. As we have seen, no reductive account of a truthmaker or a TSB-satisfying supervenience base is consistent with Truthmaker or TSB. So there must be a non-reductive truthmaker or supervenience base for *that Fido is possibly black*.

---

[11] Some (e.g., Hazen 1976; Cresswell 1990) argue that a full-blown reduction of *de re* modality requires possible worlds. If they are right, this is an additional reason to conclude that this chapter's attacks on possible worlds reductions undermine all reductions of *de re* modality.

I suppose that this must involve Fido's having an irreducible modal property, such as *being possibly black* or *being accidentally brown*.

So Truthmaker and TSB suggest that there are at least some irreducible modal properties. Moreover, those properties are suggested in order to play a role in making true. Thus, Truthmaker and TSB suggest that those properties are not suspicious.

Truthmaker is false if and only if there are truths without truthmakers. Those of us who deny Truthmaker think that there are such truths. But even those of us who think that some truths lack truthmakers ought also to think that some other truths have truthmakers. Consider the truth *that Merricks exists*. I am a truthmaker for this truth. (That truth seems to be appropriately about me and, moreover, if I exist, then that truth must be true.) Similarly, given that I exist, there is a TSB-satisfying supervenience base for *that Merricks exists*.

So even those of us who deny Truthmaker and TSB ought to say that some truths have truthmakers. And we ought to say that at least some truths have a worldwide local supervenience base. These claims are far less controversial than full-blown Truthmaker or TSB. Yet these claims commit us to exactly the same sort of *de re* modality as do Truthmaker and TSB. So these claims get us *de re* modality of a sort that cannot be accommodated by a broadly Quinean reduction of *de re* modality (§III).

Indeed, this sort of *de re* modality cannot be reduced at all. I say this partly because, as was noted above (§II), we should endorse the basic lines of the Truthmaker- and TSB-based attack on abstract worlds reductions of this sort of modality even if we are not truthmaker theorists or TSBers. And I say this partly because I share the nearly universal conviction that Lewis's possible worlds do not exist and, as a result, that Lewis's reduction of *de re* modality fails. So all of us—whatever we think of Truthmaker and TSB—should conclude that there is irreducible *de re* modality.

6

PRESENTISM

Presentism was briefly described in earlier chapters. But since it is about to take centre stage, a more detailed description is in order. So this chapter begins by contrasting presentism with its chief rival, eternalism. It then criticizes a couple of attempts to reconcile presentism with Truthmaker and TSB, going on to argue that no such reconciliation is possible. Rather than a mark against presentism, so the chapter argues, this is a reason to deny Truthmaker and TSB. The chapter closes with some comments on modality.

I. Presentism and Eternalism

Eternalists say that objects existing at past (and future) times really do exist. So, for example, eternalists say that not only do you and I exist, but so do dinosaurs and the entire parade of Roman emperors. Presentists deny that dinosaurs exist. Ditto for the Caesars. Of course, presentists believe that some things exist—namely, those things that exist at the present time. In fact, the standard definitions of 'presentism' are all some variant or other of the claim that *everything* exists at the present time (see, e.g., Bergmann 1999; Crisp 2004; Keller 2004; Lewis 2004; Markosian 2004; Rea 2003; Sider 2001: 11).

But these standard definitions, even though they get at something important, fail to get at what separates presentism most fundamentally from eternalism. I say this, in part, because eternalism itself is arguably consistent with the claim that everything exists at the present time. After all, eternalism is, at least arguably, consistent with nothing ever existing; so eternalism is consistent with nothing existing that does not also exist at present; so eternalism is consistent with the claim that everything exists at the present time.[1]

There is another reason that I say that these standard definitions fail to get at what separates presentism most fundamentally from eternalism. It is that these definitions do not even allude to what, in my opinion, does thus separate presentism from eternalism. I think that presentism and eternalism differ most fundamentally with respect to the nature of time and, relatedly, with respect to what it is to exist at a time (and to have properties at a time). As we shall see, the paradox of change brings these differences into stark relief.

Let us approach the paradox of change by way of another paradox, a paradox predicated on David Lewis's (1986) account of possible worlds. Consider the view that an entity exists in multiple Lewisian worlds not (as Lewis himself would have it) by having counterparts in them, but instead by being wholly and entirely located in them. According to this view, multiple

---

[1] Suppose there are necessary entities. Then we should say that eternalism is arguably consistent with nothing *contingent* existing. This is enough to conclude that eternalism is arguably consistent with everything existing at the present time, since necessary entities presumably exist at all times. (If necessary things are 'outside time', then they do not exist at the present time; but even presentism is supposed to allow that things outside time do not exist at the present time.)

   Assuming that eternalism is consistent with nothing (contingent) ever existing, eternalism is also consistent with the definition of 'presentism' that says that, *always*, everything exists at the present time. But eternalism is not consistent with the definition of 'presentism' that says that, *necessarily*, everything exists at the present time. But this latter definition entails that presentism is a matter of necessity. So presentism itself might be inconsistent with this definition, since presentism might turn out to be contingent.

worlds 'overlap' at that one entity. This view says that I exist in more than one world much as I might exist, when standing in an intersection, in more than one street.

Suppose that in one world I am cuboid. Suppose that in another I am spherical. (For the sake of illustration, grant that it is possible for me to have these shapes.) Add to these suppositions the overlap view just described, and we get the result that one thing—me—is both cuboid and spherical. This is impossible. So, as Lewis (1986: 198–209) rightly argues, the overlap view must go.

The impossibility involved in overlap gets going only given Lewis's picture of modality. That is, the modal paradox of overlap is an artefact of Lewis's modal realism, which treats other possibilities as akin to other places. This sort of paradox-generating overlap makes no sense given a view of modality that abandons Lewis's possible worlds.[2]

Given eternalism, other times are akin to other places. To 'exist at a time' is to be located at a particular time. As a result, an object's existing wholly and entirely at more than one time means that the object is wholly located at multiple times. It means, in other words, that these multiple times 'overlap' at that object. Given eternalism, I wholly exist at more than one time much as I might exist, when standing in an intersection, in more than one street.

Suppose that at one time I am cuboid, at another spherical. Then, given eternalism, two times overlap at one me, a 'me' who is both cuboid and spherical. This is impossible. Thus the paradox of change. The eternalist must find a way out of this

---

[2] Such a view might abandon possible worlds altogether. Or it might take worlds to be abstracta. Paradox-generating overlap makes no sense given abstract worlds, because my 'existing in' two abstract possible worlds—i.e., in two propositions—is nothing like my existing in two streets by standing in their intersection. Rather, for me to 'exist in an abstract possible world' is for me to be such that, were that world actual (true), then I would exist. Something similar goes for my 'having a property in a world' (see van Inwagen 1985).

paradox.[3] But the eternalist's 'way out' is not the point here.
The point here is, instead, that this paradox gets going only
given the eternalist's picture of other times.

The paradox of change is an artefact of eternalism, which
treats other times as akin to other places. Paradox-generating
overlap makes no sense given presentism. For presentists do
not think an object exists at two times much as that object
might exist, when standing in an intersection, in two streets.
This is because presentists do not think that other times are
like other places. Indeed, presentists should deny that past
times and future times exist at all.[4] (Presentists can endorse
the existence of past and future 'abstract times'; see the next
section.)

Presentists deny that past times exist. Nevertheless, presentists should insist that many existing objects *did exist*. I am not
sure what account presentists should give of an object's having
existed. They might give no account at all. Or they might
reduce an object's having existed to its having primitive 'past-
directed' properties, such as *having existed*.[5] Or they might
endorse some other account of an object's having existed. But
there is one account that they cannot endorse. Presentists

[3] The most obvious way out is to deny that I *wholly* exist at various times. The
eternalist can say, instead, that I only *partially* exist at various times. I partially
exist at various times by having numerically distinct parts, one or another of
which wholly exists at (and only at) each of those times. Thus I have 'temporal
parts'.

[4] Presentists need not say that ordinary, everyday claims such as the following
are false: 'there was a time when the Soviet Union existed'. Instead, presentists
can say that while such claims apparently refer to a time, they do not really do so,
any more than ordinary claims about 'the average plumber' really refer to some x
such that x is an average plumber. Presentists could take 'there was a time when
the Soviet Union existed' as saying something along the lines of, e.g., for some
number n of years, the Soviet Union existed n years ago.

[5] What is the difference between giving no account of an object's having
existed and giving an account in terms of irreducible past-directed properties? It
is the same as the difference between giving no account of what it is for there to
be no hobbits (which I favor) and giving an account in terms of an object's having
the irreducible property of *being such that there are no hobbits* (which I oppose).

cannot reduce an object's having existed to it (or its temporal parts) being located at a region called a 'past time'.

Something similar goes with respect to properties had 'at past times'. I was a child at some past time. Presentists may not reduce this to my (or my temporal part's) being a child and my (or my temporal part's) being located at a region called a 'past time'. But they could, for example, reduce this to my having the property of *having been a child*.

Suppose that I do have the property of *having been a child*. Add that I have the property of *not being a child*. My having these two properties does not lead to an overlap of times with its ensuing paradox. Nor is there anything else paradoxical about my having these two properties. So, given presentism, there is nothing paradoxical about my being a child at a past time and failing to be a child at the present time. More generally, given presentism, there is nothing paradoxical about change.

Presentists and eternalists alike say that those things that exist at the present time really do exist and, moreover, that properties had at the present time really are had. Thus one might think that, while presentism and eternalism part ways with respect to other times, they agree about the nature of the present time and, relatedly, agree about what it is to exist (and have properties) at the present time. But they do not agree about these things. Indeed, their differences with respect to the nature of, and existence at, the present time are as important as their differences with respect to the past and the future.

To begin to see why I say this, note that those who reject Lewis's many universes should not start with Lewis's theory of modality and his multiverse and then 'shave off' all the worlds but our own, leaving us with just one possible (and actual) world. Again, those who reject the Lewisian multiverse should not agree with Lewis that to possibly exist is to exist in a possible world, parting ways with him only by insisting that our universe is the only possible world. For they would then be committed to the view that the things that exist (and the way things are) are the only things that could possibly exist (and are the only way things could possibly be). Such a view implies that everything is necessary.

Now consider a view that starts with the eternalist's picture of time and existence at a time, and then 'shaves off' the past and the future, leaving only a thin (instantaneous?) slice called 'the present'. This view agrees with eternalism that existing at a time—at any time, past, present, or future—is like being located at a place. But, unlike eternalism, this view says that while objects exist at the present time, they exist at no other times, since there are no other times at which to be located. Such a view implies that everything is instantaneous.[6]

This view is not presentism. Presentists deny that everything is instantaneous; they think that many objects not only exist, but also have existed and will exist. But I can see why some might think this view is presentism. They think this view is presentism because they (wrongly) ascribe to presentists the eternalist's claim that *to exist at a time* is to be located at some super-thin slice of being. But presentists should no more accept this than the non-Lewisian should accept that to possibly exist is to be located in some universe. In fact, I think presentists

---

[6] With this in mind, consider these remarks from Lewis:

Second solution: the only intrinsic properties of a thing are those it has at the present moment. Other times are like false stories; they are abstract representations, composed out of the materials of the present, which represent or misrepresent how things are. When something has different intrinsic properties according to one of these ersatz other times, that does not mean that it, or any part of it, or anything else, just *has* them—no more so than when a man is crooked according to the *Times*, or honest according to the *News* .... In saying that there are no other times, as opposed to false representations thereof, [this solution] goes against what we all believe. No man, unless it be at the moment of his execution, believes that he has no future; still less does anyone believe that he has no past. (1986: 204)

Lewis seems to be describing presentism, combined with an endorsement of abstract times of the sort discussed in the next section. But his closing objection has purchase only on the view that everything is instantaneous, which is the view just noted in the text, but is not presentism.

should deny that there is anything at all—much less some super-thin slice of being—that is the present time, just as they should deny that there are past times or future times. (But they can affirm the existence of 'abstract times'; see the next section.)

Of course, presentists insist that there are objects that *exist at the present time* (or, equivalently, that *presently exist*). Since they do not believe in a region called the 'present time', presentists cannot reduce *existing at the present time* to being located at that region. I think presentists should, instead, say that *existing at the present time* just is *existing*. Thus, given presentism, if something exists, then, obviously enough, it exists at the present time. So, given presentism, since everything exists, everything exists at the present time. This is what is right about the standard definitions of presentism.[7]

II. Abstract Times

Truthmaker demands a truthmaker for:

(1) The Trojans were conquered.

Eternalists can offer the state of *the Trojans' being conquered*. Given eternalism, that state is just as real as (e.g.) *Neptune's orbiting the sun*. Of course, both of these states are far from

---

[7] Here is an objection commonly encountered in conversation, if only rarely in print—but see Lombard 1999. If 'exists' means *presently exists*, then of course the only things that exist (in that sense) are those that exist at the present time. If, instead, 'exists' means *exists at some time or other*, then of course there are things that exist (in that sense) that do not exist at the present time. Presentists and eternalists disagree only verbally, one using 'exists' in the first way, the other in the second. For compelling refutations of this objection, see Sider 1999, 2006 and Crisp 2004. All I want to add here is that, at most, this objection clouds what is at stake in the debate between presentism and eternalism with respect to the catalogue of existing entities. But presentism and eternalism disagree over more than that catalogue. Presentism and eternalism disagree over the nature of time and over what it is to exist at a time, disagreements untouched by this objection.

us. But distance from us—whether temporal or spatial—is irrelevant to a state's fitness for truthmaking. Eternalists can similarly appease TSB with respect to (1), insisting that there really are some Trojans who are being conquered.[8]

Presentists deny that the state of *the Trojans' being conquered* exists. Moreover, they deny that there are any Trojans who are being conquered. So presentists cannot embrace the eternalist's ways of reconciling (1)'s truth with Truthmaker and TSB. More to the point, some have charged that there is no way for presentists to reconcile the truth of claims like (1) with Truthmaker and TSB. Those who levy this charge include David Armstrong (2004: ch. 11), David Lewis (1999*a*: 207), Theodore Sider (2001: 35–42), and Michael Tooley (1997: 234–40).

Published versions of this charge focus on the role of necessitation in both Truthmaker and TSB. So let us start there. Suppose (1)—the Trojans were conquered—is true. But, so the charge goes, (1)'s truth is not necessitated by what exists at the present time or by the properties that each thing exemplifies at the present time. So, given presentism, nothing necessitates (1). Thus, if presentism is true, (1) fails to have a truthmaker, and (1) lacks a worldwide local supervenience base. And so do many other truths about the past.[9]

---

[8] Eternalists deny that propositions change in truth-value. So I suppose that eternalists take (1) to express a proposition that asserts that the Trojans were conquered *at some time* t (or *before* t). And so, to be a bit more precise than I was in the text, I suppose that eternalists will say that that proposition is made true by the state of the Trojans being conquered *at* t (or *before* t).

[9] As we saw in the preceding section, eternalists and presentists disagree about how to analyse *existing at the present time*. But this disagreement does not preclude agreement about *which things* exist at the present time. For example, presentists and eternalists agree that the state of affairs of *the Trojans' being conquered* does not presently exist. This is enough to generate the Truthmaker- and TSB-based objection to presentism. (Compare: The Lewisian and the actualist disagree about how to analyse *actually existing*, but they agree that horses actually exist and unicorns do not.)

In all that follows, I assume that presentists will not respond to Truthmaker and TSB by denying that there are any truths about the past. But some have flirted

A presentist might reply to this charge by way of *abstract times*. My account of these 'times' builds on the following points from Chapter 4 (§III). A proposition p is *maximal* if and only if, for every proposition q, p entails q or, instead, p entails q's denial. Presentists must say that the true maximal proposition has not always been true. So, since which world is actual does not change over time, presentists must deny that to be the actual world is to be the true maximal proposition. More generally, presentists must deny that maximal propositions are possible worlds.

Presentists should say, instead, that maximal propositions are abstract times. And they should add that *being present*, for an abstract time, just is *being true*.[10] Moreover, they should say that a maximal proposition is a *past* time just in case that proposition *was true*. Similarly, a *future* time is a maximal proposition that *will be true*.

Let us add that something *exists at* an abstract time if and only if, necessarily, if that time is present (i.e., true), then that something exists. In other words, something exists at an abstract time if and only if that time entails that that something exists. Similarly, something has a property at an abstract time if and only if that time entails that that something has that property. Finally, a claim is true at an abstract time if and only if that time entails that claim.

(Many abstract times are such that, necessarily, if they are present (true), I exist. So I exist at many abstract times. So does every other persisting entity. Nevertheless, everything exists

with something like this response. Thus Jan Lukasiewicz (1967), partly motivated by something like Truthmaker, denies that there are any truths about past events unless those past events have presently existing effects. Michael Dummett (1978) also seriously considers a view along these lines. See also Markosian 1995.

[10] Eternalists, unlike presentists, should not identify times with maximal propositions or *being present* with such a proposition's *being true*. For that would imply, given eternalism, that only one time has ever been or ever will be present. Eternalists should, instead, identify possible worlds with maximal propositions, and *being actual* with such a proposition's *being true*.

at the present (abstract) time. This is because, for any existing thing x, it is true that x exists. So, for all existing entities x, the true maximal proposition—that is, the present time—entails *that x exists*. And so, given our account of existing at an abstract time, everything exists at the present time.)

Recall the standard Truthmaker- and TSB-based objection to presentism, which says that, given presentism, there is nothing to necessitate the truth of claims like the following:

(1) The Trojans were conquered.

Abstract times suggest the following straightforward response. *That the Trojans are being conquered* is true at a past (abstract) time. That is, a maximal proposition that was true—that is, a time that was present—entails *that the Trojans are being conquered*. Necessarily, if this maximal proposition (exists and) *was true*, then (1) itself *is true*. Thus the state of affairs of this maximal proposition's having been true (or having been present) is a presently existing thing that necessitates (1).

This straightforward response has two flaws. First, it is needlessly complex. If we can say that the relevant maximal proposition *was true*, then we can say that some non-maximal proposition *was true*. We could say, for example, that the proposition *that the Trojans are being conquered* was true. We could then add that (1)—which says that the Trojans were conquered—is necessitated by the past truth of *that the Trojans are being conquered*. This is simpler than the solution invoking abstract times.

Of course, relying on the past truth of *that the Trojans are being conquered* feels like a cheat. This is at least partly because to say that a claim *was true* is tantamount to saying that it stands in the *having once exemplified* relation to *being true*. And grounding the truth of (1) in another proposition's relation to *being true* seems to be cheating. But then grounding the truth of (1) in the past truth of an abstract time (i.e., maximal proposition) is also cheating. Thus we have the second flaw of the above straightforward abstract-times reply to Truthmaker and TSB.

But suppose we could give an account of the *pastness* of an abstract time that did not rely on that time's standing in a relation to *being true*, a relation like *having once exemplified*. Suppose, further, that this account of pastness worked only for maximal propositions and so not for comparatively minimal propositions like *that the Trojans are being conquered*. Such an account would have neither of the flaws of the 'straightforward response', which said that *that the Trojans were conquered* is necessitated by a certain maximal proposition's having been true.

Thomas Crisp (2007) develops just such an account. Crisp's account turns on an '*earlier than*' relation that holds between some abstract times and the abstract present time. The relata of this relation, being abstracta, presumably have always existed and will always exist. So it cannot be that one of the relata existed before—that is, earlier than—the other did. Again, in the most straightforward senses of 'earlier' and 'later', Crisp's *earlier than* relation does not hold between an earlier existing time and a later existing time. Rather, that relation is a technical device introduced by Crisp, a device that he treats as primitive.

Crisp says that for an abstract time to be 'past' is for it to stand in this *earlier than* relation to the present time. So Crisp does not define pastness in terms of *was true*. Moreover, Crisp does not say that a time stands in the *earlier than* relation to the present time *because* it was true. Rather, he says, the *earlier than* relation holds as a matter of brute fact. And since his *earlier than* relation holds only among times, abstract times do not seem to be a needless complication whose work could be done more economically by propositions like *that the Trojans are being conquered*.

A time is past, according to Crisp, if and only if it stands in the *earlier than* relation to the time that is present. So, in order for an abstract time to be past, some other abstract time must be present—that is, true. Crisp thinks that a time is partly made true by, among other things, familiar objects such as Fido having familiar properties such as *being brown*. He adds that a time is also partly made true by the existence of other times and their being related to that time by *earlier than*.

So a time's being past, according to Crisp, just is the primitive *earlier than* relation's holding between it and the present time. Moreover, a time's being future, again according to Crisp, just is the primitive *earlier than* relation's holding between the present time and it. Following Crisp (2007), let the 'ersatz B-series' be the whole array of abstract times—one of which is present (i.e., true)—related to one another by the *earlier than* relation.[11]

Crisp's explicit aim is to block the standard Truthmaker- and TSB-based objection to presentism. Necessarily, Crisp would say, if the ersatz B-series exists and has the features it has, then it is true that the Trojans were conquered. In this way, the ersatz B-series necessitates (1): the Trojans were conquered. This blocks the standard objection that, when it comes to (1), presentism cheats. For recall that this objection says that, given presentism, nothing necessitates (1).

If there is no ersatz B-series, then no such series necessitates truths about the past. Thus Crisp's solution is not available to those who take abstract times and the ersatz B-series in the same way that some take possible worlds: namely, as mere heuristic devices rather than as *bona fide* objects. But if we grant Crisp the existence of the ersatz B-series as he has described it, then we should agree that Crisp has achieved his stated aim. He has blocked the standard Truthmaker- and TSB-based objection to presentism by providing something that necessitates truths about the past.

---

[11] Merely possible abstract times—those maximal propositions that are not and never have been and never will be true—are not part of the ersatz B-series at all.

But we have seen that Truthmaker and TSB should demand more than that, for each truth, there is something that necessitates it. For example, defenders of Crisp's solution must agree that Crisp's primitive *earlier than* relation is not suspicious, since that relation plays an essential role in making claims like (1)—not to mention the present (abstract) time—true. That the *earlier than* relation is not suspicious is a second cost of Crisp's solution, a cost in addition to the existence of the ersatz B-series itself.

And here is one more cost. Any past abstract time *was true*. Lest his view collapse into the doubly flawed straightforward response above, Crisp cannot rely on that time's having been true in accounting for what makes it a past time, that is, in accounting for what makes it stand in the *earlier than* relation to the present. Presumably, then, Crisp should say that the 'accounting' runs in the other direction.[12] He should analyse *was true* in terms of his primitive *earlier than* relation. Thus he reduces at least one ordinary temporal feature—*was true*—to the elements of the ersatz B-series.

I think that this pushes Crisp toward reducing temporality as a whole to the ersatz B-series. And something else pushes a reduction of the past (and future) to the ersatz B-series, if the ersatz B-series really is to reconcile presentism with Truthmaker and TSB. For Truthmaker and TSB require even more than that something or other necessitates each truth, and does so without relying on suspicious properties. They also require that what a truth is appropriately *about* necessitates that truth (Ch. 2, §§II–III; Ch. 4, §VI). Thus, reconciling presentism with Truthmaker and TSB by way of the ersatz B-series requires that truths about the past be appropriately

---

[12] Or Crisp might claim that there is no account to be given. That is, he might claim that it is a brute synthetic necessity that a maximal proposition stands in the primitive *earlier than* relation to the present time if and only if that proposition was true.

about the ersatz B-series, which I think suggests a reduction of the past to that series.

Sometimes it is obvious what a truth is about, in the sense of 'about' central to Truthmaker and TSB. For example, I think it is obvious that *that Merricks exists* is thus about me. (That is, I think this is obvious if we grant to Truthmaker and TSB that there is the relevant sort of *aboutness* in the first place.) But it is not always obvious what a truth is thus about.

For example, *that there is water in the bucket* is, arguably, thus about the bucket's containing H_2O molecules. Surely this would not have been obvious to our pre-molecular-theory forebears. Or suppose that knowledge is analysed as true belief caused by a process with features F, G, and H. Then *that someone knows that it is raining* is appropriately about a person's having the belief that it is raining caused by a process with features F, G, and H. But even so, it is not obvious that this claim is thus about a person's having a belief caused in this way.

So, in the sense of 'about' that is crucial to Truthmaker and TSB, it is not always obvious what a truth is about. Nevertheless, we can sometimes be confident that a truth is *not* thus about some suggested entity's existence or its having certain suggested properties. For example, *that there is water in the bucket* is not about God's willing that there is water in the bucket. And—lest the presentist be able to satisfy Truthmaker and TSB far too easily—*that the Trojans were conquered* is not about *being true*'s being exemplified by *that the Trojans were conquered*.

Reconciling presentism with Truthmaker and TSB by way of the ersatz B-series requires that truths about the past be appropriately about the ersatz B-series. But I say that claims about the past are not thus about the ersatz B-series. Again, I say that claims like *that the Trojans were conquered* are not about a primitive relation holding between one maximal proposition and another. This seems to me as clear an example of a claim's failing to be about something that allegedly necessitates it as we could want.

Claims about the past are not appropriately about the ersatz B-series. As a result, Crisp's account of what would, given presentism, necessitate truths about the past cannot be turned into an account that fully reconciles presentism with Truthmaker and TSB. More generally, any full reconciliation of presentism with Truthmaker and TSB in terms of abstract times succeeds only if truths about the past are not merely necessitated by, but are also appropriately about, the existence and features of abstract times. And I deny that claims like *that the Trojans were conquered* are thus about abstract times.

III. Lucretianism

In *On the Nature of the Universe*, Lucretius says:

Again, when men say it *is* a fact that Helen was ravished or the Trojans were conquered, we must not let anyone drive us to the admission that any such factual event *exists* independently of any object, on the ground that the generations of men of whom these events were accidents have been swept away by the irrevocable lapse of time. For we could put it that whatever has taken place is an accident of a particular tract of earth. (1994: 21)

Lucretius is not replying to the Truthmaker- or TSB-based objection to presentism. Nevertheless, his comments suggest a reply. Let L be the land upon which burnt the topless towers of Illium. The 'Lucretian' says that L has the property of *being such that the Trojans were conquered*. L's having that property necessitates the truth of:

(1) The Trojans were conquered.

Our sun will eventually enter a red giant phase and envelop the whole earth. (Bummer.) No more L. But even then, (1) will still be true—that is, it will still be true that the Trojans were conquered—and the charge of cheating will re-emerge. At least from a cosmic perspective, L's being such that the Trojans were conquered is a mere stopgap measure.

Roderick Chisholm says: 'If there once was a philosopher who drank the hemlock and who no longer exists, then there always will be something—for example, the property blue—which once *was* such that there *is* a philosopher who is drinking the hemlock' (1990: 416). Taking a page from Chisholm, Lucretians could say that (1) is made true by an abstractum's having the property of *being such that the Trojans were conquered*. Or they could say instead that the whole universe has that property.[13] Both options promise everlasting grounding for (1), and so permanent Lucretian solutions.

Lucretians say that the universe (or an abstractum or …) presently has past-directed properties, properties like *being such that the Trojans were conquered*. Because the universe now has such properties, they say, the properties that things presently have necessitate truths about the past. Thus Lucretianism provides the resources to block the standard Truthmaker- and TSB-based objection to presentism, the objection that, given presentism, nothing necessitates truths about the past.

Presumably, its defenders think not only that Lucretianism *can* block the standard objection to presentism, but also that Lucretianism *is required* to block that objection. That is, Lucretians think that their past-directed properties are essential to blocking that objection. But if they are right, then the having of past-directed properties has no non-past-directed

[13] As we saw in Ch. 2 (§IV), this is the gloss that Bigelow (1996: 45) puts on Lucretius. Its substantive implications are that there is a universe, that the universe will always exist, and that once the universe has the relevant property, it will never lose it. Lucretius (1994: 21) himself suggests that the relevant property might be had by 'the space' in which an event occurred. If spaces do exist and are everlasting, we can add them to the universe and abstracta as candidates for being the bearers of Lucretian properties.

supervenience base. For if it did, then that non-past-directed supervenience base would itself necessitate truths about the past.[14] And then that base itself would constitute a thoroughly non-Lucretian way to block the standard Truthmaker- and TSB-based objection to presentism.

Presumably, Lucretianism implies that (at least some) past-directed properties have no non-past-directed supervenience base. If the having of a property does not supervene on the having of other properties (or relations), then that property is primitive or irreducible or fundamental (see Ch. 3, §II). By invoking past-directed properties that fail to supervene on the non-past-directed, Lucretianism is thereby committed to some primitive past-directed properties.[15]

I think that many of the primitive and non-supervening past-directed properties required by the Lucretian—properties like *being such that the Trojans were conquered*—are suspicious. That is, I think it is a cheat to rely on these properties, especially when exemplified by things like the universe or an abstractum, to satisfy Truthmaker and TSB.[16]

I suspect that my objection will be endorsed by many truth-maker theorists and TSBers (see, e.g., Armstrong 2004: 145–6). But it is not clear to me that they should endorse it. For Lucretianism's distinctive past-directed properties are natural denizens of the truthmaker theorist's and TSBer's property menagerie, which already includes not only primitive modal

---

[14] Here is why. If the exemplification of past-directed properties supervenes on something else, then that something else necessitates the exemplification of those properties. Those properties, *ex hypothesi*, necessitate truths about the past. Necessitation is transitive. So that which necessitates that which necessitates truths about the past thereby necessitates truths about the past.

[15] A 'sparse' Lucretian could say that most past-directed properties supervene on, and are reduced to, combinations of a few irreducible past-directed properties. But all Lucretians need some irreducible past-directed properties.

[16] I do not say that all past-directed properties are suspicious: e.g., it is not clear to me that only a cheater would claim that *that Merricks was a child* is grounded in my having the irreducible property of *having been a child*.

properties (Ch. 5), but also primitive properties like *being such that there is nothing more in the universe* (Ch. 3).

Perhaps there is no principled way to rule out irreducible past-directed properties without also ruling out, among others, an irreducible 'nothing more' property. Then truthmaker theorists and TSBers have no right to object to Lucretian properties. From the vantage-point of Truthmaker and TSB, those properties may be unobjectionable.

Even so, truthmaker theorists and TSBers should not be completely happy with Lucretianism, and not just because they are, as a rule, hostile to presentism. For Truthmaker and TSB demand that a truth is necessitated by that which it is *about* (Ch. 2, §§II–III; Ch. 4, §VI). So Lucretianism satisfies Truthmaker and TSB only if truths apparently about the past are appropriately about the world's presently having certain irreducible properties.

With this in mind, consider this definition from Chisholm, which follows his comments quoted above:

D5 There existed an x such that x was F=Df. There exists a y which was such that there exists an x such that x is F. (1990: 416)

Chisholm here offers a *definition* of what it is for something that existed to have been a certain way. Given this definition, Chisholm would say that (1) *means* that something or other has the Lucretian property of *having been such that the Trojans exist and are being conquered*. So, presumably, he would say that (1) is appropriately about something or other's having that property.

Along similar lines, A. N. Prior says:

… the fact that Queen Anne has been dead for some years is not, in the strict sense of 'about', a fact about Queen Anne … if it is about anything, what it is about is not Queen Anne—it is about the earth, maybe, which has rolled around the sun so many times since there was a person who was called 'Anne', reigned over England, etc. (1968: 19)

These passages from Chisholm and Prior illustrate what Lucretianism must say about claims about the past, if Lucretianism is to render presentism consistent with Truthmaker and TSB. Lucretianism must say that claims about the past are appropriately about presently existing objects and some irreducible properties that those objects now exemplify.

As I noted in the previous section, it is not always obvious what (if anything) a truth is about, in the sense of 'about' relevant to Truthmaker and TSB. But sometimes it is clear that a truth is not thus about something, even something that necessitates that truth. For example, a proposition is not typically thus about God's willing that it be true. Nor is a proposition typically thus about the mere existence of a world-bound entity.

With this in mind, I say that *that Queen Anne has been dead for some years* is not about some entity that will exist and have the relevant irreducible property for as long as it is true that Queen Anne has been dead.[17] Nor is (1), which says that the Trojans were conquered, about (e.g.) the property of *being blue* having the primitive property of *being such that the Trojans were conquered*. Therefore, the sort of Lucretianism that would reconcile presentism with Truthmaker and TSB is false.

IV. Choose Presentism

Consider once again:

(1) The Trojans were conquered.

---

[17] I say that there is no existing entity (or entities) to which *that Queen Anne has been dead for some years* stands in the *aboutness* relation, that relation that is part and parcel of Truthmaker and TSB. I do not deny, however, that in a different and more familiar sense of 'about', *that Queen Anne has been dead some years* is 'about something'—obviously, it is 'about Queen Anne'. But this no more implies that Queen Anne exists than a ghost story's being 'about ghosts' implies that ghosts exist (see Ch. 2, §III).

I think that, in the sense of 'about' that is crucial to Truthmaker and TSB, (1) is not about *presently* existing objects or the *presently* exemplified properties of such objects. Presentism therefore implies that (1) is not thus about *any* existing objects or *any* properties of such objects.

This implication reinforces the point that the ersatz B-series and Lucretianism fail to reconcile presentism with Truthmaker and TSB. For both the ersatz B-series and Lucretianism succeed only if (1) is about existing objects (such as, e.g., the ersatz B-series) or the properties (such as, e.g., Lucretianism's past-directed properties) those objects exemplify. But this implication does not merely reinforce that point. This implication also shows that no possible view can reconcile presentism with Truthmaker and TSB. This is because Truthmaker says that every truth is about some existing things. And TSB says that, for every truth, there exist some things, or there are some properties had by some existing things, that that truth is about.[18]

Given the truth of claims like (1), presentism cannot possibly be reconciled with Truthmaker and TSB. So either presentism has to go, or Truthmaker and TSB have to go. I would reject Truthmaker and TSB even if they did not clash with presentism (Ch. 3, §V; Ch. 4, §VIII). But they do clash with presentism.

---

[18] Presentism accords no more reality to merely future objects and events than it does to those that are merely past. And so some have objected that, given truths about the future, presentism cannot be reconciled with Truthmaker and TSB (see, e.g., Lewis 1999a: 207 and Armstrong 2004: 145–6).

With this in mind, consider this argument from Rhoda, Boyd, and Belt (forthcoming). Presentism is true; so there are no truthmakers for contingent truths about the future; so there are no such truths; so God lacks foreknowledge of what will contingently happen. This argument fails because Truthmaker is false. Moreover, if both Truthmaker and presentism were true, there would be no contingent truths about the past—so God would also lack knowledge of what did contingently happen. As far as truthmaking and presentism go, foreknowledge is no more problematic than is knowledge of the past. But I doubt that opponents of exhaustive divine foreknowledge also want to oppose exhaustive divine knowledge of the past.

And this is a further reason to reject them, since eternalism is false and presentism is true.[19]

One reason to reject eternalism is that it, unlike presentism, implies that dinosaurs and woolly mammoths and the fourth-millennium human outposts on Mars and the heat-dead universe all exist. Eternalism implies that the gladiator battles in the Coliseum rage on, each of your eight great-great-grandfathers is taking his first steps, and humans are crossing an ice bridge from Asia to North America for the first time. Because eternalism implies these things, we should reject it.

Do not misunderstand. Eternalism does not imply that the gladiator battles rage on *and are located at the present time*. Rather, eternalists say that while those gladiator battles do indeed exist and rage on—and so can, even today, serve as truthmakers for *that some gladiator battles raged on*—they are located only at past times. The Martian outposts, on the other hand, are located only at future times. But, as with the gladiator battles, eternalists say that those outposts really do exist. That is why the outposts can, given eternalism, serve this very day as truthmakers for claims like *that there will be human outposts on Mars*.

Eternalists insist that the gladiator battles and the Martian outposts and so on are not located at the present time. But, even keeping this point clearly in mind, eternalism still implies, among other things, that the gladiator battles rage on and Martian outposts really do exist. And I find the view that gladiator battles rage on and Martian outposts really do exist

[19] Even those who endorse just the mere possibility of presentism should reject Truthmaker and TSB. For if presentism is possible, then it is possible for there to be truths with neither truthmakers nor a TSB-satisfying supervenience base. This latter possibility is inconsistent with Truthmaker and TSB. I point this out only because some argue that presentism is inconsistent with Special Relativity (e.g., Balashov and Janssen 2003). But presumably we are not entitled to claim that Special Relativity is *necessarily* true. So even defenders of this argument should conclude at most that presentism is actually false—thus the presentism-based threat to Truthmaker and TSB remains.

no more believable than David Lewis's (1986) view that some pigs really do fly and some donkeys really do talk. And I do not find Lewis's view believable at all, not even when I keep clearly in mind Lewis's point that the flying pigs and the talking donkeys are *not located in the actual world*.

Unlike eternalism, presentism is believable. Moreover, presentism seems to be the ordinary and natural way to think about time. Thus John Bigelow: 'I am a presentist: nothing exists which is not present. I say that this was believed by everyone, both the philosophers and the folk, until at least the nineteenth century; it is written into the grammar of every natural language; and it is still assumed in everyday life even by philosophers who officially deny it' (1996: 36). Presentism is the common-sense view, and its rivals merit an incredulous stare.

And consider this argument for presentism. First, if you know that you existed yesterday, then presentism is true. Second, you know that you existed yesterday. Therefore, presentism is true. This argument is clearly valid. And few will deny that you know that you existed yesterday. I do recognize, however, that the conditional first premiss needs a bit of defence.

That defence begins by returning to the idea that eternalists believe that other times are akin to other places. And so existing at multiple times, for the eternalist, is like being spread out in space. A spatially extended object typically has numerically distinct parts located at the distinct places it occupies. And so the natural thing for an eternalist to say is that a temporally extended object has numerically distinct parts located at the distinct times it occupies—and thus has temporal parts.

Suppose you have temporal parts. Then, presumably, you have a temporal part existing from 2005 to 2010. That 2005–10 'segment' of you has many of the properties you have during that five-year period. For example, if you fly across the Atlantic six times during those five years, so does that segment. If you have a full head of red hair from 2005 to 2010, so does that segment. When you entertain thoughts during those five years, so does that segment.

Focus on this last example. It is bad enough that, from 2005 to 2010, there are at least two thinkers (i.e., you and that segment) thinking each of your thoughts, rather than, as we would normally suppose, just one (i.e., you). But it gets worse. For suppose you think to yourself, 'I existed in the year 2000'. Your segment too thinks this. You think this truly, the segment falsely.[20] Unfortunately, you cannot tell whether you are the person who has existed for decades, or instead the segment, which has existed only since 2005. After all, everything seems to you just as it seems to that segment, and vice versa.

Again, 'what it is like' to be you from 2005 to 2010 is identical with 'what it is like' to be that segment from 2005 to 2010. And so I conclude that—if you have temporal parts—you do not know whether you are that five-year-long segment or instead the lifelong person. And so you do not know that you existed in the year 2000. Of course, this argument generalizes. If you have temporal parts, then you do not know that you existed in the year 2000, or in the year 2001, or even yesterday (see Merricks 2001: 47–53 and 98–9; Olson 1997: 166).[21]

---

[20] Your belief that you existed in the year 2000 is true; the segment's belief that it then existed is false; so, by the indiscernibility of identicals, there must be two beliefs here. But the temporal parts picture is that there is *just one belief*, had by the person in virtue of being had by the segment. Thus another problem for the temporal parts view.

Some might object that 'I' refers only to the person; therefore, even when the temporal segment thinks 'I existed in the year 2000', it thereby thinks that the person of which it is a part then existed; and so it thinks truly. Suppose that this objection is correct about the way 'I' works (but it is not correct; see Merricks 2003*b*). Still, this objection fails to touch the point that 'what it is like' to be me from 2005 to 2010 is 'what it is like' to be my 2005–10 stage. And so I cannot tell, during that interval, whether I—i.e., this thinking thing—am a lifelong person or a five-year segment. Nor can I tell, if this objection is right about the way 'I' works, whether my uses of 'I' refer to me, i.e., to this thinking thing. (See Merricks 2001: 50.)

[21] The eternalist could try to block this argument by saying that none of our temporal parts exist long enough to have beliefs. But this renders temporal parts

As I noted above, it is natural for an eternalist to say that persisting objects have temporal parts. And I have argued in much more detail elsewhere that if eternalism is true, then persisting objects do have temporal parts.[22] So let us assume that if eternalism is true, then you have temporal parts. But we have just seen that if you have temporal parts, you do not know that you existed yesterday. So we can conclude that if eternalism is true, you do not know that you existed yesterday. Therefore, if you do know that you existed yesterday, then eternalism is false. And if eternalism is false, then presentism is true (see Merricks 2006). This concludes my defence of the premiss introduced above: if you know that you existed yesterday, then presentism is true. [23]

V. An Objection

I say that truths entirely about the past lack truthmakers and a TSB-satisfying supervenience base. But Thomas Crisp objects:

unable to fully account for change, which is a significant cost. (Suppose I am at one time thinking of my childhood, at another not….) Moreover, by denying that one has a 2005–10 temporal segment, one denies that every combination of parts composes another thing; but then one must reject Sider's (1997; 2001: 120–39) influential argument in favour of temporal parts. (For criticisms of that argument, see Merricks 2005.)

[22] I argue (Merricks 1999) that eternalism entails that persisting objects have temporal parts. (And I argue (Merricks 1995) that presentism precludes persisting objects from having temporal parts.) The 'stage theory' version of temporal parts, defended by Sider (1996, 2001) and Hawley (2001), is immune to this section's objection to temporal parts. But stage theory is false because it identifies a person with an instantaneous stage and thereby, so I would argue, denies that persons persist at all (see Merricks 2003c).

[23] Another argument for presentism, in addition to the arguments of this section, is that presentism alone allows for genuine change. That is, presentism alone permits the direct having of a property by something and then, later, the absolute lacking of that property by that same thing (Merricks 1994; Hinchliff 1996; Crisp 2003). This is connected to presentism's claim that propositions can change in truth-value (Ch. 4, §III; Ch. 6, §II). For if an object O had property F, and then later lacked it, *that* O *is* F changed in truth-value.

It does seem exceedingly strange, though, that truths about the past and future should be [brute] truths [i.e., truths that violate Truth-maker and TSB]. The truth that I have hair is not brute—worlds in which it is false that I have hair will represent various of my properties differently than does the actual world. A hundred years from now it will be true that I had hair. Isn't it odd that *that* truth should be brute? (2003: 239–40)

Simon Keller (2004: 91–3) raises the same objection.

Crisp and Keller are not simply repeating the Truthmaker- and TSB-based objection to presentism. For even if Truth-maker and TSB are false, the truth of *that the Trojans are being conquered* supervened on the features of some Trojans. But if the truth of *that the Trojans are being conquered* supervened on being, so too—according to Crisp and Keller—should the truth of *that the Trojans were conquered.* For Crisp and Keller would say that these truths, differing merely in tense, ought to be treated alike when it comes to truthmaking.

If *that a man is climbing a golden mountain* were true, it would be made true by a man and a golden mountain and how one was related to the other. Contrast this with the truth of *possibly, a man is climbing a golden mountain.* Nearly all of us can agree that this latter claim is not made true by any man's relation to any golden mountain. After all, that claim is true even though no golden mountain exists. Therefore, when it comes to truthmaking, *possibly, a man is climbing a golden mountain* should not be treated like *that a man is climbing a golden mountain.*

Given presentism, *that a man climbed a golden mountain* is not at all like *that a man is climbing a golden mountain.* It is more like *possibly, a man is climbing a golden mountain.* This should be clear from what has been said about presentism already. And it is reinforced by the fact that the presentist can say that *that a man climbed a golden mountain* is more perspicuously presented as *WAS, a man is climbing a golden mountain,* where *WAS* is a tense operator much as *possibly* is a modal operator (see Sider 2001: ch. 2; Lewis 2004).

At any rate, the modality of *possibly, a man is climbing a golden mountain* makes all the difference with respect to what (if anything) is required to make it true. And if presentism is true, the same goes for a claim's tense. Crisp's and Keller's objection does not acknowledge this point. On the contrary, Crisp's and Keller's objection presupposes that certain cases are alike with respect to 'making true' that, given presentism, are not alike at all. So their objection presupposes that presentism is false. No presentist should be moved by their objection.

VI. Modality Redux

Perhaps some truths that are apparently about the past really are appropriately about a presently existing object's presently having certain properties. Consider *that Merricks was a child.* Arguably, that truth is about my presently having a property like *having been a child.* And so, arguably, the Lucretian approach works in cases like this one. But cases like this are the exception, rather than the rule. Truths apparently about the past are typically not about a present object's now being a certain way. For example, *that the Trojans were conquered* is not about a present object's now being a certain way.

Similarly, some modal truths may be about actual objects and the properties they actually exemplify. For example, *that Fido is possibly black* may be about the actual Fido's actually exemplifying *being possibly black.* But other modal truths are not like this. Suppose, for example, that there are fundamental particles. Now consider the truth *that there might have been a dozen more fundamental particles.* This is not about any actual objects or the properties such objects actually have.

Truthmaker theorists and TSBers might reply that all such claims are about possible worlds and what those worlds are like. But in Chapter 5 I argued against reducing modality to possible worlds and their features. Indeed, I argued, such reductions are especially misguided as attempts to reconcile truths of modality with Truthmaker and TSB, since those reductions are particularly untenable given Truthmaker and TSB.

One might claim that *that there might have been a dozen more fundamental particles* is about the universe's having the property of *being such that there might have been a dozen more fundamental particles*. This seems to me on a par with Lucretianism, and thus heir to Lucretianism's woes: the relevant properties are suspicious, and, moreover, the truth in question is not about the universe exemplifying the relevant (suspicious) irreducible property.

At any rate, I conclude that *that there might have been a dozen more fundamental particles* is true, but is not appropriately about any existing entities or the properties that such entities have. Given this conclusion, Truthmaker, which says that all truths are thus about existing entities, is false. And TSB is false as well, since TSB says that all truths are thus about which entities exist and which properties those entities have.

7

SUBJUNCTIVE CONDITIONALS

COUNTERFACTUALS of freedom and ungrounded dispositional conditionals are among the most notorious violators of Truthmaker and TSB. This chapter examines these, and other, subjunctive conditionals. It argues that at least some subjunctive conditionals give us yet another reason to deny Truthmaker and TSB. The chapter closes by noting which truths have truthmakers or a TSB-satisfying supervenience base.

I. Molinism

The sixteenth-century Jesuit Luis de Molina (1988) thought that free human actions could not be determined by anything, not even by God. Nevertheless, Molina claimed, God knows truths about what each and every possible human would freely do in each and every possible situation. Thus, according to the 'Molinist', God knows some counterfactuals of freedom. An example of a counterfactual of freedom is:

(1) If Curley had been offered a $35,000 bribe, he would have freely taken it.

According to Thomas Flint (1998: 122–3), the principal objection to Molinism is that counterfactuals of freedom cannot be true. They cannot be true, according to this objection, because nothing could *ground* them if, as Molinists insist, freedom is incompatible with determinism. As I shall now argue, this objection to Molinism is equivalent to the objection that counterfactuals of freedom cannot be true because, given incompatibilism, they lack truthmakers and fail to satisfy TSB.[1]

Given incompatibilism, Curley's desires, intentions, and character do not necessitate the truth of (1). This alone, so defenders of the grounding objection charge, makes them unfit to ground (1)'s truth (see, e.g., Adams 1987: 80). This charge makes sense only if necessitation is necessary for grounding. So let us assume that it is.[2]

Robert Adams tells us the following about Francisco Suarez, an early defender of Molina:

... according to Suarez, [a possible agent] *c* has a property (a *habitudo*, as Suarez puts it) which is either the property of being a possible agent who would in *s* freely do *a*, or the property of being a possible agent who would in *s* freely refrain from doing *a*. *c* has one of these properties.... God [knows] what *c* would do in *s*, because God knows which of the two properties *c* has. (1987: 81–2)

Suarez would claim that (1) is grounded by Curley's having the property of *being such that had he been offered a $35,000 bribe, he would have freely taken it*.[3]

---

[1] Both defenders (e.g., Hasker 1989: 24) and opponents (e.g., Craig 2001) of the grounding objection to Molinism have equated it with the charge that no counterfactual of freedom is true because they all lack truthmakers.

[2] Given this assumption, we can conclude that the grounding objection is not concerned with *epistemic* grounding, since an epistemic ground need not necessitate. For example, my experience of seeming to see a tree epistemically grounds—i.e., in some sense justifies or warrants—my belief that there is a tree, but it does not necessitate that there is a tree. Some counterfactuals of freedom might have epistemic grounds: e.g., my knowledge of Curley's character might be epistemic grounds for my belief that (1) is true even if that knowledge does not necessitate (1).

[3] Here the relevant property is had by Curley, whom we are assuming exists. But Suarez talks of 'possible agents'. Since a merely possible agent does not exist, it has no properties whatsoever, much less properties of the sort that Suarez

As Adams recognizes, Suarez has a leg up on those who try to ground (1) in Curley's character, since 'Suarezian properties' necessitate their respective counterfactuals. Nevertheless, Adams denies that Suarez is ultimately successful. For Adams denies that Suarezian properties can properly ground the relevant counterfactuals. In the parlance of this book, Adams deems those properties to be suspicious.[4]

There are really two points here. The first is that what grounds a truth, if it is to satisfy defenders of the grounding objection, cannot rely on certain properties; in other words, certain alleged properties are judged, by the grounding objection, to be 'suspicious'. This first point is part of my case that the demand for grounding is one and the same as the demand for either truthmakers or a TSB-satisfying supervenience base. The second point is that, as Adams says, Suarezian properties are suspicious, and so the Suarezian attempt at grounding fails.

A defence of this second point starts by noting that some properties—perhaps *having negative charge* or the relation of *identity*—admit of no analysis, and so are primitive. But others are analysable, and so not primitive. And *being such that had he been offered a $35,000 bribe, he would have freely taken it* surely seems to be the sort of property that, if it existed in the first place, would be analysable. And likewise for other Suarezian properties. So, whatever we might say of Suarezian properties if they turned out to be analysable, I think that if Suarezian properties are primitive, they definitely should be judged to be suspicious.

---

invokes. In light of this, perhaps a Suarezian should attribute (analogues of) the Suarezian properties to individual essences, which exist necessarily. An individual essence of Curley, e.g., is a property that Curley exemplifies essentially and, moreover, that cannot possibly be exemplified by anything other than Curley (see Plantinga 1974: 70).

[4] Adams (1987: 82) says: 'I do not think I have any conception, primitive or otherwise, of the sort of *habitudo* or property that Suarez ascribes to possible agents with respect to their acts under possible conditions.'

With this in mind, suppose that an agent's having a Suarezian property were necessitated by the exemplification of other properties, properties that constituted an analysis of that Suarezian property. Then the exemplification of those other properties would necessitate whatever is necessitated by the agent's having the Suarezian property, including the relevant counterfactuals of freedom. This would render the Suarezian property superfluous. So there is no reason for the Molinist to introduce Suarezian properties unless an agent's having a Suarezian property is not itself necessitated by the exemplification of properties that constitute an analysis of that Suarezian property.

That is, there is no reason to introduce Suarezian properties unless they are not analysed in terms of other properties.[5] So it should be no surprise that Adams (1987: 81–2) says that, according to Suarez, 'there is nothing either internal or external to c, except the property itself, which would make or determine c to have one of these [Suarezian] properties rather than the other'. So let us conclude that if there are Suarezian properties, they have no analysis, and so are primitive. Given this conclusion, I think we should join Adams in deeming them to be suspicious. And I think all defenders of the grounding objection would agree.

We have been seeking a ground for this counterfactual of freedom:

(1) If Curley had been offered a $35,000 bribe, he would have freely taken it.

One might suggest that it is grounded by the state of affairs of *God's believing (1)*. After all, because God cannot have false beliefs, this state necessitates the truth of (1). Thus, as a ground of (1), this state enjoys Suarezian superiority over, for

---

[5] If a property has an analysis, its exemplification is necessitated by the exemplification of (at least some of) the properties involved in its analysis (Ch. 3, §II; Ch. 6, §III).

example, Curley's character. Moreover, this state is free of the defects of the Suarezian solution. For it is not constituted by any suspicious properties. Its only constituents are God, the relation of *believing*, and (1) itself.

Theists who hold that some counterfactuals of freedom are true can say that, since God is omniscient, God believes those counterfactuals. Therefore, as the example just given illustrates, theists can offer a state of affairs that necessitates every allegedly true counterfactual of human freedom, and does so without relying on any suspicious properties. But the moral here is not that, given theism, counterfactuals of freedom are easily grounded. It is, instead, that there is more to grounding than necessitation without reliance on a suspicious property.

There must be more. For, first, surely God believes a counterfactual of freedom because it is true, not—as implied by the attempt to ground (1) in God's believing—the other way around. Second, and relatedly, the relevant counterfactual is not appropriately about God's believing; instead, it is about what this or that free agent would do in this or that circumstance. I think that these two points rule out grounding (1) in God's believing (1). And they suggest that a ground for a counterfactual of freedom must be that which that counterfactual is appropriately about (see Ch. 2, §III).

That which grounds a counterfactual of freedom must be what that counterfactual is in some way *about*. And, as we saw above, it must *necessitate* that counterfactual. Moreover, as we also saw above, it cannot be constituted by, or otherwise rely on, *suspicious properties*. In light of all of this, I conclude that the claim that counterfactuals of freedom are true only if grounded is equivalent to the claim that they are true only if they have truthmakers, or at least a TSB-satisfying supervenience base.

The grounding objection is the principal objection to Molinism. So many who object to Molinism deny that counterfactuals of freedom have truthmakers or the relevant supervenience base. But, perhaps surprisingly, most of those who support

Molinism deny this as well. Alvin Plantinga (1985), Richard Otte (1987), Thomas Flint (1998), Alfred Freddoso (1988), Rod Bertolet (1993), and William Lane Craig (2001) all seem to think that counterfactuals of freedom cannot be grounded. (They take this as a reason to reject not Molinism, but rather the demand for grounding.)

By and large, Molinists and their opponents agree that counterfactuals of freedom lack truthmakers and a TSB-satisfying supervenience base. This consensus should not be surprising. For counterfactuals of freedom are about what someone *would do* in a non-actual, counterfactual situation. So I think that, in the relational sense of 'about' that plays a central role in Truthmaker and TSB, they are not about what exists or what properties are actually exemplified. This alone shows that true counterfactuals of freedom would violate Truthmaker, since Truthmaker says that all truths are thus about what exists (Ch. 3, §V). They would likewise violate TSB, since TSB says that all truths are thus about what there is and the properties those existing things actually have (Ch. 4, §VIII).

Counterfactuals of freedom are about what an agent *would do*, rather than about how things *are*. Such counterfactuals, therefore, are not about the properties (actually) had by an (actually existing) agent. So they are not about an agent's having Suarezian properties. But then an agent's having Suarezian properties cannot ground such counterfactuals. For a truth must be about what grounds it. Thus we have a new reason to reject the Suarezian attempt to ground counterfactuals of freedom.

A Suarezian might remind us that what a claim is about, in Truthmaker and TSB's sense of 'about', is not always obvious. To return to an example from the last chapter, *that there is water in the bucket* is, arguably, thus about the bucket's containing H_2O molecules. But this is not obvious to those not acquainted with molecular theory, not even if they are well acquainted with water. Similarly, the Suarezian might insist that, although it is not obvious, counterfactuals of freedom really are about, in Truthmaker and TSB's sense of 'about', properties that an agent actually has.

My first reply to this claim is to remind us that even though what a truth is thus about may not be obvious, there are still clear cases of a truth's failing to stand in that *aboutness* relation to something. (At least, there are clear cases just as long as we can make sense of the relevant sort of *aboutness*—and so can make sense of Truthmaker and TSB—in the first place.) And I say that among the clear cases are any true counterfactual of freedom and the actual having of a Suarezian property.

And I have a second reply. For starters, suppose that I am a truthmaker for *that a human exists*. So that truth stands in Truthmaker's *aboutness* relation to me. But it is not obvious, at least not to those who do not know of my existence, that that proposition is thus about me. Along similar lines, one need not know of my existence to understand that proposition. So one need not know of my existence to know what, in another and more familiar sense of 'about', that proposition is about. In this other sense, that proposition is 'about humans'. And it would be 'about humans' even if no humans existed, even if there were no humans to stand in an *aboutness* relation to it.

These two senses of 'about' were first contrasted in Chapter 2 (§III). I shall now introduce a new claim about how these two distinct senses of 'about' are related to one another, a claim not made earlier in this book. I think that *that a human exists* stands in the *aboutness* relation to me because, first, it is—in the more familiar sense of 'about'—'about humans', and second, I am a human. Likewise, suppose that *that there is water in the bucket* stands in the *aboutness* relation to the bucket's containing H_2O molecules. This is presumably a result of the following two points. First, in the more familiar sense of 'about', that proposition is 'about water in the bucket', and second, the water in the bucket is reduced to or is analysed as or is somehow constituted by H_2O molecules.

With all of this in mind, I add that there must be some connection along the lines of the connections just noted between what a proposition is 'about' in the non-relational, more familiar sense and that to which that proposition stands in Truthmaker's and TSB's relation of *aboutness*. And I deny that there is the relevant connection between claims about what an object *would do* and the properties the object *actually has*. For example, what an object *would do* is not reduced to (or analysed in terms of or somehow constituted by) the properties that object actually has. And so the Suarezian solution fails.

Consider once more:

(1) If Curley had been offered a $35,000 bribe, he would have freely taken it.

Suarezians might object that (1) asserts exactly that Curley has the primitive property of *being such that had he been offered a $35,000 bribe, he would have freely taken it*. They might object, that is, that (1) is misleadingly phrased in counterfactual terms, but is *in the familiar non-relational sense of 'about'*, about Curley's having that property. If so, then presumably they can claim that (1) also stands in the *aboutness* relation to Curley's having that property.

I reply that, in general, we can grasp a particular Suarezian property only by way of seeing that it is the property that, if had by a certain agent, would make the relevant counterfactual of freedom true. So, for example, the only sense we can make of *being such that had he been offered a $35,000 bribe, he would have freely taken it* is that it is a primitive property that, when had by Curley, grounds the truth of (1). With this in mind, suppose for *reductio* that (1) asserts exactly that Curley has that primitive property. Then all we know about that property is that it is the property that, if had by Curley, makes true a claim that asserts exactly that Curley has just that property. But then I say that our understanding of that Suarezian property evaporates.

Look at it this way. Suppose that there is a claim other than (1) that asserts exactly that Curley has a Suarezian property (other than the property that (1) asserts that he has), a property that, if had by Curley, makes that claim true. I have no idea what that property is. And neither do you. But this case is perfectly analogous to (1), if (1) asserts exactly that Curley has the Suarezian property that, if had by Curley, makes (1) true. Again, if we take (1) to assert just that Curley has a certain Suarezian property—and if all we know about that property is that it is the property that makes (1) true—our understanding of that Suarezian property evaporates. And once our understanding of Suarezian properties evaporates, so too does our understanding of the Suarezian solution.

It is better for the Suarezian to deny that (1) merely asserts that Curley has some primitive Suarezian property, even if the having of that property would make (1) true. It is better for the Suarezian to say, instead, that (1) wears its meaning on its face, and is indeed 'about what an agent would do in a certain non-actual circumstance'. I think that we can understand (1), thus interpreted. So we can understand the claim that there is a particular primitive property, the having of which by Curley grounds the truth of (1). And so we can, at least partially, grasp that primitive property. But then, of course, the Suarezian solution is vulnerable to my original objection: (1) does not then seem to stand in the appropriate *aboutness* relation to an agent's actually having any property.

To return to the main line of argument, Molinism is inconsistent with both Truthmaker and also TSB. Because I think that Truthmaker and TSB are false for reasons having nothing to do with Molinism, I do not think that this inconsistency is a reason to reject Molinism. But—if Molinism itself is motivated—this inconsistency does give us yet another reason to reject Truthmaker and TSB.

The principal motivation for Molinism is that it delivers the strongest form of divine providence consistent with incompatibilism and human freedom (see Flint 1998: 75–6; Hasker 1986: 546). Molinism says that God knows what free creatures would do in every possible situation. Thus, from among the possible worlds consistent with the true counterfactuals of freedom, God can bring about any world that he wishes, down to the smallest detail.[6]

Some of us believe not only in incompatibilism and human freedom, but also in the strongest sort of divine providence consistent with our beliefs about freedom. We should be Molinists. We should conclude that there are true counterfactuals of freedom. This is a new reason (for us) to deny both Truthmaker and TSB. For true counterfactuals of freedom lack both truthmakers and also a TSB-satisfying supervenience base.

II. Counterfactuals of Determined Action

I shall now argue that something akin to counterfactuals of freedom leads to a new reason for everyone—not just those who share the Molinist's motivating convictions—to reject Truthmaker and TSB. So this argument will not presuppose theism. Nor will it presuppose incompatibilism or, for that matter, compatibilism. Instead, it presupposes only that in at least some non-actual situations, at least some human actions would be determined.

---

[6] Suppose it is true that if S were in situation C, then S would freely do A. Then God does not actually have the ability to create a world in which S is in C, but fails to do A—even if a world in which S is in C but fails to do A is possible. This feature of Molinism allows Plantinga (1974) to argue that, possibly, God cannot actualize any possible world in which free agents do no wrong, even though some such worlds are indeed possible.

If at least some human actions would be determined, then at least some *counterfactuals of determined action* are true. For example, suppose that if Curley were offered a $35,000 bribe, then it would be determined that he accepts that bribe. Then the following counterfactual of determined action is true:

(1*) If Curley had been offered a $35,000 bribe, he would have taken it.

Some counterfactuals of determined action are true. Let us suppose, for the sake of argument, that (1*) is one of these true counterfactuals. It is tempting to add that (1*) is grounded by whatever necessitates it. But this is too hasty. Necessitation alone is not sufficient for grounding. For example, your left thumb necessitates—but your thumb does not ground—Fermat's Last Theorem. Likewise, God's believing (1*) necessitates (1*), but God's believing (1*) does not ground (1*).

A ground does not merely necessitate its truth. A ground is also what its truth is appropriately *about*. So (1*) is grounded by what necessitates it only if (1*) is thus about what necessitates it. But I do not think that (1*) is thus about the most salient alleged necessitators of determined action. For example, I do not think that (1*) is thus about the laws of nature or the past. Moreover, I do not think that (1*) is thus about the way anything actually was or is. Instead, (1*) is about what Curley *would do* in a non-actual situation.

Some might object that (1*) is not really about what Curley *would do*, but is, instead, about the way that Curley *in fact is*. In particular, some might object that (1*) simply asserts something about (an aspect of) Curley's character. And if we add that Curley's character necessitates (1*), then they can say that his character grounds (1*).

Given their commitment to incompatibilism, Molinists must deny that an agent's character necessitates a counterfactual of freedom. But since (1*) is a counterfactual of *determined* action, even Molinists can allow that Curley's character necessitates (1*). Moreover, the idea that (1*) asserts that Curley has a certain character is probably not subject to my earlier objection to the conjecture that (1), a counterfactual of freedom, asserts that Curley exemplifies a Suarezian property. For, in contrast to that conjecture involving Suarezian properties, I think that we have at least some sense of the character that, according to the idea we are here considering, (1*) attributes to Curley. For example, we know that that character is not overscrupulous and puritanical. So I conclude that the idea that Curley's character grounds (1*) should be taken seriously.

I shall return to that idea in the next section. Specifically, I shall return to the claim that (1*) simply asserts that Curley has a particular character. In that same section, we shall also consider a similar claim about dispositional conditionals. And we shall see that both claims are false. But, for now, simply assume that (1*) asserts that Curley would do something in a counterfactual situation, as opposed to that he has a certain sort of character. Then—in light of the previous section's argument for the conclusion that claims about what an agent *would do* fail to stand in Truthmaker's and TSB's *aboutness* relation to that agent's actual properties—I conclude that (1*) does not stand in the *aboutness* relation to Curley's character. And, therefore, Curley's character does not ground (1*).

We are assuming, for now, that (1*) asserts that Curley *would do* a certain thing, if things were otherwise. Given this assumption—and, again, in light of the previous section's argument—I conclude not only that (1*) does not stand in Truthmaker's and TSB's *aboutness* relation to Curley's character, but also that (1*) does not stand in that relation to anything's actually having certain properties (or actually performing certain actions, etc.). But this means that (1*) cannot be reconciled with Truthmaker or TSB. For both Truthmaker and TSB imply that (1*) is thus about what makes it true, and, moreover, that only existing things, and (for TSB) existing things having actual properties, can make a claim true.

Of course, the reasoning here applies not merely to (1*), but to all counterfactuals of determined action. All such counterfactuals fail to be appropriately about what actually exists and which properties things actually have. No such counterfactuals can therefore accommodate the grounding objection or Truthmaker or TSB. But surely some counterfactuals of *determined* action are true. This is a reason for all of us—not just incompatibilists committed to divine providence—to deny Truthmaker and TSB.

III. Dispositional Conditionals

Glass *G* is fragile. And, let us also assume, the following is true:

(2) If *G* were struck, then *G* would shatter.

There is, without a doubt, an important connection between *G*'s fragility and the truth of (2). In fact, according to Gilbert Ryle, to say that *G* is fragile *just is* to say that (2) is true. Again, according to Ryle, *G*'s fragility is *nothing more than* the truth of (2).

Ryle says:

When we describe glass as brittle, or sugar as soluble, we are using dispositional concepts, the logical force of which is this. The brittleness of glass does not consist in the fact that it is at a given moment actually being shivered. It may be brittle without ever being shivered. To say that it is brittle is to say that if it ever is, or ever had been, struck or strained, it would fly, or have flown, into fragments. To say that sugar is soluble is to say that it would dissolve, or would have dissolved, if immersed in water. (1949: 43)

Ryle says that to attribute a disposition like fragility or solubility to something is merely to affirm a subjunctive conditional. So, according to Ryle, to attribute such a disposition to an object is not to attribute a feature to that object. With respect to those who say otherwise, Ryle laments: 'There still survives the preposterous assumption that every true or false statement either asserts or denies that a mentioned object or set of objects possesses a specified attribute' (1949: 120). It should come as no surprise that truthmaker theorists and TSBers are unhappy with Ryle (see, e.g., Armstrong 2004: 2–3 and Lewis 1999*a*: 207). And I shall return to the Truthmaker- and TSB-based objection to Ryle below. But I want to begin with a different objection.

Ryle's account of dispositions entails that an object's having a disposition like fragility absolutely guarantees that the relevant subjunctive conditional is true. (For only given that guarantee could an object's having that disposition be the very same thing as the truth of that conditional.) But—here is the objection—it is possible for an object to have such a disposition even though the relevant conditional is false.

Consider this example from Lewis:

A sorcerer takes a liking to a fragile glass, one that is a perfect intrinsic duplicate of all the other fragile glasses off the same production line. He does nothing at all to change the dispositional character of his glass. He only watches and waits, resolved that if ever his glass is struck, then, quick as a flash, he will cast a spell that changes the glass, renders it no longer fragile, and thereby aborts the process of breaking. So his finkishly fragile glass would not break if struck—but no thanks to any protective disposition of the glass itself. Thanks, instead, to a disposition of the sorcerer. (1999*b*: 138)

Suppose *G* is the glass beloved of the sorcerer. Then although *G* is fragile, (2)—if *G* were struck, then *G* would shatter—is false. So we have a counterexample to Ryle's conditional account of fragility.

It is well known that examples like Lewis's, examples of so-called finkish dispositions, undermine Ryle's account of dispositions.[7] Less widely appreciated is that they undermine accounts diametrically opposed to Ryle's. An account inspired by Quine illustrates this point. Here is Quine on dispositions generally and solubility in particular:

Each disposition, in my view, is a physical state or mechanism. A name for a specific disposition, e.g. solubility in water, deserves its place in the vocabulary of scientific theory as a name of a particular state or mechanism. In some cases, as in the case nowadays of solubility in water, we understand the physical details and are able to set them forth explicitly in terms of the arrangement and interaction of small bodies. Such a formulation, once achieved, can thenceforward even take the place of the old disposition term, or stand as its new definition. (1974: 10)

This first part of the Quinean account of dispositions implies that *G*'s fragility amounts to *G*'s having a 'structural' property. The second part of the Quinean account tells us that dispositional conditionals are (perhaps misleading) ways to assert only that an object has the relevant property. Here is Quine again:

At an uncritical level the usual paraphrase of the disposition idiom is an intensional [i.e., subjunctive] conditional. To say that a body is soluble in water is to say that it *would* dissolve if it *were* in water. … there is no denying that in its bumbling way this intensional conditional somehow conveys the force of the dispositional idiom. (1974: 9; see also Quine 1966: 72–3)

At a couple of points above, I have argued that a subjunctive conditional, in virtue of being about the way things *would be* in a counterfactual situation, is not appropriately about the way things *actually are*. But Quine would disagree. At least, Quine says that dispositional conditionals are about the way a thing actually is. He says that each such conditional, in its 'bumbling way', asserts exactly that something actually has the relevant structural property.

---

[7] Finkish dispositions were introduced by C. B. Martin, who used them to undermine Rylean accounts of dispositions (see Martin 1994: 8 n. 2 and Lewis 1999*b*: 133).

But I object to Quine's account of dispositional conditionals. For it implies that an object's having a structural property absolutely guarantees that the relevant dispositional conditional is true. (For only given that guarantee could that dispositional conditional assert exactly that the object has that structural property.) And—here is my objection—it is possible for an object to have a structural property even though the relevant dispositional conditional is false.

For example, Lewis's sorcerer shows that, possibly, *G* has the relevant structural property and the following is false:

(2) If *G* were struck, then *G* would shatter.

This proves not only that *G*'s fragility cannot be reduced *à la* Ryle to (2)'s truth, but also that (2) cannot be, as Quine would have it, a roundabout way of saying that *G* has the structural property of fragility.

Lewis's sorcerer shows that, given Quine's view that fragility is a structural property, *G* could be fragile and (2) false. Indeed, Lewis's sorcerer shows that, given almost any view of fragility, *G* could be fragile and (2) false. This holds even if, for example, fragility is a brute disposition or a 'power' (see Heil 2004; Molnar 2003; Martin 1993). So I think that, however we take fragility, we should conclude that (2) does not assert that *G* is fragile. More generally, we should conclude that dispositional conditionals do not assert that something has the relevant disposition.

We now have the resources to show that an objection from the last section fails, an objection that, when it was originally introduced, I simply set aside. That objection was that the following counterfactual of determined action is nothing more than a roundabout way to assert that Curley has a certain sort of character:

(1*) If Curley had been offered a $35,000 bribe, he would have taken it.

Let Curley be as corrupt as you please. This is consistent with the existence of a sorcerer who would—the very instant that Curley was offered a bribe and before Curley could respond in any way—change Curley into someone who would refuse every bribe. So no matter what Curley's character was like, (1*) could be false. Thus (1*) cannot assert just that Curley has a certain character. Nor, more generally, can any other counterfactual of determined action assert merely that an agent has a certain character.[8]

Once more, consider:

(2) If *G* were struck, then *G* would shatter.

As Lewis's sorcerer shows, *G* could be fragile but (2) false. So *G*'s fragility does not *necessitate* (2). And this implies, of course, that the state of affairs of *G's being fragile* cannot be a truthmaker for (2). It also implies that *G*'s having the property of *being fragile* fails to provide a supervenience base for (2). Indeed, I shall now argue, (2)—which we are assuming is true—has no truthmaker or TSB-satisfying supervenience base at all.

As Lewis's example shows, (2) is true only if there is no sorcerer disposed to keep *G* from shattering. Therefore (2) entails the following negative existential:

(3) There is no sorcerer who would keep *G* from shattering, were *G* to be struck.

---

[8] As will become clear below, these considerations threaten the claim that (1*) has a truthmaker (or TSB-satisfying supervenience base). But they do not threaten the claim that (1*) is determined. For suppose that there is no sorcerer of the relevant sort and that, necessarily, if Curley has the character he has and there is no such sorcerer, then (1*) is true. I think that this is enough for (1*) to be determined. But it is not enough to get us a truthmaker for (1*). For none of this implies that there is something that, by its mere existence, necessitates that there is no such sorcerer, and so none of this implies that there is something that, by its mere existence, necessitates (1*).

If (2) has a truthmaker, then that truthmaker, by its mere existence, necessitates the truth of (2). Therefore that truthmaker, by its mere existence, necessitates the truth of all claims entailed by (2). (2) entails (3). So if (2) has a truthmaker, then that truthmaker, by its mere existence, necessitates the truth of (3).

There might be some entity that, by its mere existence, necessitates the truth of (3). One example might be the state of affairs of *(3)'s being true*. Another might be the state of *God's believing (3)*. But neither of these is a truthmaker for (2). And there might be entities that seem at first glance to be truthmakers for (2), such as the state of *G's being fragile*. But none of those entities necessitates (3). And I deny that there is any entity that is, first, a truthmaker for (2), and second, necessitates, by its mere existence, the truth of (3).[9] But, since (2) entails (3), any truthmaker for (2) would have to necessitate, by its mere existence, the truth of (3). So (2) has no truthmaker at all.

Similarly, suppose, for the sake of argument, that (2) satisfies TSB. Then the existence and properties of actual objects that

---

[9] I do not say that all negative existentials fail to be necessitated by the mere existence of entities (or by their having properties) other than propositions' having truth-values, God's believings, and so on. Consider *that there is no wizard who has kept Merricks from ever existing*. I, by my mere existence, necessitate this negative existential. But, for what it is worth, I do not think that I am a truthmaker for this negative existential, since I do not think it is appropriately about me.

Frank Jackson (1994: 32) endorses the following 'entailment principle': if *p* and *q* are contingent, and *p* entails *q*, then *p*'s truthmaker is also *q*'s truthmaker. Armstrong (2004: 10–12) also endorses this principle—at least just so long as neither *p* nor *q* has any conjuncts that are necessary. Jackson's and Armstrong's entailment principle is false if I am right that the truthmaker for *that Merricks exists* is not a truthmaker for *that there is no wizard who has kept Merricks from ever existing*.

And even if I am wrong about this, Jackson's and Armstrong's entailment principle is still false. The state of affairs of *proposition* p*'s exemplifying the property of being true* is a truthmaker for *that proposition* p *exemplifies the property of being true*. But it is not a truthmaker for *p*, even though *that proposition* p *exemplifies the property of being true* entails *p*. Similarly, the state of *God's believing* p is a truthmaker for *that God believes* p. But it is not a truthmaker for *p*, even though *that God believes* p entails *p*.

make up (2)'s TSB-satisfying supervenience base necessitate the truth of (2). So those objects and their properties necessitate all that (2) entails, including (3). But I do not think that there is a TSB-satisfying supervenience base for (2) that also necessitates the truth of (3). But if there were a TSB-satisfying supervenience base for (2), it would necessitate the truth of (3). So (2) does not satisfy TSB.

In general, that *A* would manifest a disposition *D* in condition *C* entails that there is no sorcerer who, if *A* were in *C*, would keep *A* from manifesting *D*. And so all dispositional conditionals—not just (2)—entail negative existentials. Moreover, the candidates for being the truthmakers or the TSB-satisfying supervenience bases for those dispositional conditionals fail to necessitate the negative existentials that those conditionals entail. Thus the above argument surrounding (2) and (3) generalizes. In general, dispositional conditionals lack truthmakers and a TSB-satisfying supervenience base. But some dispositional conditionals are true. So we have a new reason to conclude that Truthmaker and TSB are false.[10]

It would be a mistake to say, instead, that we have a reason to conclude that there are no true dispositional conditionals. For the truth of (2)—the claim that if *G* were struck, then *G* would

[10] For all *p*, *p* entails *that there is no sorcerer who keeps* p *from being true*. So every truth entails some negative existential or other. Locating the negative existentials entailed by a truth is the first step in a general strategy for attacking both the claim that that truth has a truthmaker and also the claim that it satisfies TSB. But it is just the first step. For not every negative existential entailed by a truth gives us a reason to think that that truth lacks a truthmaker or a TSB-satisfying supervenience base. What we need is a negative existential that is not only entailed by that truth, but that also fails to be necessitated by every seeming truthmaker for that truth and, moreover, fails to be necessitated by what seems to be that truth's TSB-satisfying supervenience base. Dispositional conditionals do entail such negative existentials, which is why I focused on dispositional conditionals in the text. On the other hand, consider again *that there is no wizard who has kept Merricks from ever existing*. This negative existential is entailed by *that Merricks exists*. And I not only seem to be a truthmaker for *that Merricks exists*, I also, by my mere existence, necessitate that negative existential.

shatter—follows from *G*'s fragility along with there not being any entities relevantly like the meddling sorcerer. So the above considerations should lead us to deny the truth of (2) only if we are also willing to deny the truth of the relevant negative existentials. But surely *that there is no sorcerer who would keep* G *from shattering, were* G *to be struck* is true.

Upon reflection, I do not think that it should be surprising that dispositional conditionals are counterexamples to Truthmaker and TSB. For, to vary a theme played in the previous two sections, a dispositional conditional is not a claim appropriately about the way an actual thing actually is. A dispositional conditional is, instead, about the way something would be in a non-actual situation. As a result, there is nothing whose existence and features are what a dispositional conditional is about, in the sense of 'about' central to Truthmaker and TSB. So it should be no surprise that dispositional conditionals have neither truthmakers nor a TSB-satisfying supervenience base.

This section's argument against Truthmaker and TSB is even stronger than I have suggested so far. For although I am convinced by cases like Lewis's sorcerer that the fragility of *G* does not necessitate the truth of (2), the argument here does not require this. Suppose, for the sake of argument, that, necessarily, *G* is fragile if and only if (2) is true. So suppose, therefore, that *G* would not be fragile if a sorcerer formed an intention to keep it from shattering. (Thus *G*'s fragility would not be determined by its microstructure.) Even so, (2) still lacks a truthmaker and a TSB-satisfying supervenience base. This is because (2) still entails the negative existential regarding the sorcerer. Indeed, given what we are supposing for the sake of argument, the truth of *that* G *is fragile* entails that same negative existential—and so *that* G *is fragile* is yet another counterexample to Truthmaker and TSB.

Above I said I would return to the Truthmaker- and TSB-based objection to Ryle's account of dispositions. The objection, of course, is that Ryle's account fails because, on that account, dispositional conditionals violate Truthmaker and TSB. We can now dismiss this objection. For this section has argued that, no matter what account of dispositions turns out to be correct, dispositional conditionals violate Truthmaker and TSB. Nevertheless, as noted above, Ryle's account of dispositions must be rejected. For, like Quine's account of dispositional conditionals, it is inconsistent with the possibility of finkish dispositions.

IV. The Truth in Truthmaker and TSB

A version of the following argument can be found in each of the last three sections. A counterfactual—that is, a subjunctive conditional with a false antecedent—is not appropriately about the way anything *is*. (In this regard, a counterfactual is like a negative existential.) A counterfactual is, instead, about how something *would be*, had other things differed from how they actually are. As a result, true counterfactuals have neither truth-makers nor a supervenience base of the sort required by TSB.

With this in mind, return to our stock example:

(4) If Queen Elizabeth II had been born in seventeenth-century Japan, she would have been a samurai warrior.

(4) is not about how things are, but rather about how they would be, had things gone differently. So the previous paragraph's line of reasoning shows that (4)'s lacking a truthmaker or TSB-satisfying supervenience base does not tell against (4)'s truth.

Nevertheless, for all I have argued here, it could be that (4)—along with every other substantive claim along these lines—is false. Moreover, even if (4) happens to be true, none of us knows that (4) is true. So anyone who asserts (4) has done something wrong.

Even though no one should assert (4), it is still an open question whether—for all any of us knows—(4) is true. More generally, and more to the point, it is still an open question whether there is some truth or other relevantly like (4), that is, some truth or other about the career HRH would have enjoyed, had she been born in Japan 400 years ago.

Suppose that God could have sent the Queen Mother back in time just as she was going into labour with Elizabeth. Then it is possible for Elizabeth to have been born in seventeenth-century Japan. And if this is possible, then those who share the Molinist's belief in strong divine providence will insist that God knows how things would have turned out for Elizabeth-san.

So those who both believe that time travel is possible and also believe in divine providence thereby have reasons to believe that some conditional or other relevantly like (4) is true. There may be other reasons to think some such conditional is true. Alternatively, one might be able to argue that no such conditional is true. That conclusion is consistent with all I have said about Truthmaker and TSB. Again, nothing in my attacks on Truthmaker and TSB implies that (4), or some similar claim, must be true.

As far as all of this goes, I insist on only one point: it is a mistake to dismiss all substantive conditionals about how things would have gone, had Elizabeth II been born long ago in Japan, simply because 'nothing could make them true'. More generally, it is a mistake thus to dismiss any claim that is not appropriately about what exists and what properties are had.[11] For claims that are not thus about what exists and what

---

[11] Here is, at least arguably, one more example of this mistake. G. E. Moore (1903) and J. L. Mackie (1977) both assume that claims about the morally good must be grounded in (the existence and nature of) actual properties, in particular in distinctively moral properties. Moore goes on to embrace a non-natural property of the good, while Mackie denounces any such property as objectionably 'queer'. But suppose, for the sake of argument, that truths about moral goodness are about what *morally ought to be* and not about, in any good sense of 'about', what exists and which properties those existing things actually exemplify. Given that supposition, we should reject Moore's and Mackie's shared assumption. Of course, this supposition is not obviously true. But neither is it obviously false.

properties are had do not need to be 'made true' by what exists or by the properties things have.

Some might object that there is no good sense to be made of Truthmaker's and TSB's *aboutness* relation. They must conclude that there is no good sense to be made of the claim that any truth has a truthmaker or a TSB-satisfying supervenience base. Needless to say, defenders of this objection will join me in rejecting both Truthmaker and TSB. But, unlike these foes of Truthmaker and TSB, I am inclined to think that there is the relevant *aboutness* relation. For example, I think that *that Merricks exists* stands in that *aboutness* relation to me. So I think that I am a truthmaker for *that Merricks exists*.[12]

More generally, I think that truths like *that Merricks exists*, truths that really are entirely about what exists, must have truthmakers.[13] And I also think that truths entirely about the properties actually had by existing things must have a TSB-satisfying supervenience base; an example of this sort of truth is *that Fido exemplifies the property of being brown*. The truth in

---

[12] As we saw in Ch. 2 (§III), there is a familiar sense of 'about' in which every proposition is 'about something'. To understand a proposition is to know what that proposition is thus about. (*That hobbits do not exist* is thus 'about hobbits'.) Obviously enough, *that Merricks exists* is 'about Merricks' in this familiar sense. Moreover, I necessitate *that Merricks exists*. Some might object that only this—as opposed to anything involving Truthmaker's and TSB's alleged *aboutness* relation—makes me seem to be a truthmaker for *that Merricks exists*.

But there are other cases of equally intuitive truthmaking that cannot be explained away in this manner. Suppose there is a state of affairs of H_2O *molecules* $m_1 \ldots m_n$ *being related to each other in way* R, where such molecules' being thus related necessitates that there is some water. Suppose that state has its constituents essentially. Then I think we should say that that state is a truthmaker for *that some water exists*. In particular, that truth seems to be appropriately *about* that state. But this is not the familiar sense of 'about'. For one could understand *that some water exists* without knowing anything about molecules or relation R.

[13] Other truths may have—but need not have—truthmakers. (Something similar goes with respect to satisfying TSB.) Consider the disjunction *that Merricks exists or hobbits do not exist*. I myself am a truthmaker for that disjunction. So that disjunction is, in fact, about what exists (i.e., me) in the sense required by Truthmaker. But that disjunction would have been true—and truthmakerless—if I (and hobbits) had failed to exist. So it is not entirely about what exists.

Truthmaker and TSB is that some truths have truthmakers and some truths have a TSB-satisfying supervenience base. The error of Truthmaker is the claim that all truths have truthmakers, that all truths are relevantly like *that Merricks exists*. The error of TSB is the claim that all truths have a TSB-satisfying supervenience base, that all truths are relevantly like *that Fido exemplifies the property of being brown*.

8

THEORY OF TRUTH

THE correspondence theory of truth is not Truthmaker (Ch.
1, §IV; Ch. 2, §IV). But this chapter shows that the correspondence theory is committed to one of Truthmaker's false
implications. Therefore the correspondence theory is false.
Some of the correspondence theory's competitors have a similar false implication, the implication that each truth is true in
virtue of how it is related to some existing entity or entities.
The theory of truth defended in this chapter, which is that
being true is a primitive monadic property, does not have this
false implication.

I. The Correspondence Theory of Truth

In *The Problems of Philosophy*, Bertrand Russell says:

When an act of believing occurs, there is a complex, in which
'believing' is the uniting relation, and subject and objects are arranged
in a certain order by the 'sense' of the relation of believing. Among the
objects, as we saw in considering 'Othello believes that Desdemona
loves Cassio', one must be a relation—in this instance, the relation
'loving' ... When the belief is *true*, there is another complex unity, in
which the relation which was one of the objects of the belief relates
the other objects. Thus, e.g., if Othello believes *truly* that Desdemona
loves Cassio, then there is a complex unity, 'Desdemona's love for
Cassio', which is composed exclusively of the *objects* of the belief, in
the same order as they had in the belief, with the relation which was

one of the objects occurring now as the cement that binds together the other objects of the belief...

Thus a belief is *true* when it *corresponds* to a certain associated complex, and *false* when it does not. (1912: 127–8)

Russell's 'complex unity' here just is a fact, as 'fact' is understood in *The Philosophy of Logical Atomism*. So Russell claims that a belief is true when it corresponds to a fact or (in other words) to a state of affairs or to an event.

Like Russell, J. L. Austin (1979) defends a version of the correspondence theory of truth. But unlike Russell, Austin does not analyse *corresponding to* in terms of a truth-bearer's structure mirroring that of the relevant state of affairs. Here is Austin on correspondence:

'Corresponds' also gives trouble, because it is commonly given too restricted or too colourful a meaning, or one which in this context it cannot bear. The only essential point is this: that the correlation between words (= sentences) and the type of situation, event, &c., which is to be such that when a statement in those words is made with reference to an historic situation of that type the statement is true then, is *absolutely and purely* conventional. We are absolutely free to appoint *any* symbol to describe *any* type of situation, so far as being merely true goes. In a small one-spade language [the statement that] nuts might be true in exactly the same circumstances as the statement in English that the National Liberals are the people's choice. There is no need whatsoever for the words used in making a true statement to 'mirror' in any way, however indirect, any feature whatsoever of the situation or event; a statement no more needs, in order to be true, to reproduce the 'multiplicity', say, or the 'structure' or 'form' of the reality, than a word needs to be echoic or writing pictographic. To suppose that it does, is to fall once again into the error of reading back into the world the features of language. (1979: 124–5)

The truth-bearers with which Austin is concerned—namely, statements—are something like sentences in a natural language. Since we could conventionally stipulate that a simple statement corresponds to a complex state, Austin argues, a statement's structure need not mirror that of its corresponding state of affairs.[1]

Like both Russell and Austin, G. E. Moore thinks that truths correspond to facts or states of affairs or events. And, like Russell, Moore is concerned with true beliefs, not true statements. But Moore does not affirm Russell's analysis of the correspondence relation. Nor does he join Austin in positively rejecting it. In fact, Moore is completely silent about that relation's nature. This does not prevent him, however, from offering an account of truth. For Moore thinks that such an account need only refer to, not analyse, the relation of correspondence. Thus Moore says:

The relation I mean is the relation which the belief '*that I have gone away*', if true, has to the fact [or the state of affairs] '*that I have gone away*' while the name of the belief is 'The belief that I have gone away' while the name of the fact is 'That I have gone away'. We may take different views as to what the exact nature of this relation is—as to how it is to be analysed, and as to how it resembles or differs from other relations; but in merely attempting to answer these questions, we do, I think, presuppose that we are already acquainted with it—that we have it before our minds; for you cannot try to determine the nature of, or to compare with other things, a thing which you have not got before your mind. Well it seems to me that the difficulty of *defining* truth and falsehood arises chiefly from the fact that this relation, though we are all acquainted with it, has no unambiguous name; it has no *name* which is just appropriated to it alone, and which may not also be used for other relations, which are perhaps quite different from it. The moment we do give it a name, it becomes, I think, quite easy to define truth and falsehood. Let us

[1] Suppose that it is a matter of convention that a particular statement in a natural language would (if true) correspond to a certain state of affairs. Even so, it is presumably not a matter of convention that a particular belief would (if true) correspond to a certain state of affairs. This raises the possibility that Austin and Russell are merely talking past each other, one making a claim about correspondence involving true statements, the other about correspondence involving true beliefs. But I do not think that they are merely talking past each other. I think they disagree about the primary bearers of truth, and, as a result, disagree about what it is for a primary truth-bearer to correspond to something.

give it a name and see how the definition turns out. I propose to call it the relation of 'correspondence' ... Well, then, using the name 'correspondence' *merely* as a name for this relation, we can at once assert 'To say that this belief is true is to say that there is in the Universe *a* fact to which it corresponds; and to say that it is false is to say that there is *not* in the Universe any fact to which it corresponds.' (1953: 276–7)

Despite their differences regarding both the relata and the nature of *corresponding to*, Russell, Austin, and Moore would all agree that each truth corresponds to something. Moreover, all three would agree that if a truth corresponds to something, that something exists. Put otherwise, all three would agree that if that something had not existed, then that truth would not have corresponded to it.

They also seem to agree that a truth is—in some sense of 'about' or other—*about* that to which it corresponds. This is clearest in Austin, who says that a truth 'describes' that to which it corresponds (1979: 123). And it is suggested by Russell's and Moore's examples. Russell says that *that Desdemona loves Cassio* would (if true) correspond to *Desdemona's loving Cassio*, and Moore says that *that Moore has left* would (if true) correspond to the fact that Moore has left. None of these philosophers would claim, for example, that Fermat's Last Theorem corresponds to your thumb.

So Russell, Austin, and Moore all say that each truth corresponds to some existing thing that that truth is about. In fact, they seem to agree that a claim's corresponding to something that exists, something that that claim is about, is *what it is* for that claim to be true.[2] Thus they offer an analysis of *being true*, and so offer a theory of truth. But their theory of truth is false. It is false because there are some truths that are not true in

---

[2] Moore (1953: 283) is 'inclined to think' that correspondence gives us 'the very meaning of the word "truth"'. But he concedes that correspondence may be only necessary and sufficient for truth.

virtue of being related to some existing thing that that truth is about.

For example, there is no existing thing that is what *that hobbits do not exist* is about (in any good sense of 'about'), and is such that being appropriately related to it is what it is for *that hobbits do not exist* to be true; and so it goes generally for true negative existentials (Ch. 3). Moreover, it is false that there exists something that is what *that there might have been a dozen more fundamental particles* is about, much less something whose being related to that claim is what it is for that claim to be true (Ch. 6, §VI). Likewise, given presentism, for *that the Trojans were conquered* (Ch. 6). The same goes for many true subjunctive conditionals (Ch. 7). Indeed, this goes for any truth that is not about the mere existence of something (Ch. 7, §IV).

The theory of truth agreed upon by Russell, Austin, and Moore is false. So the correspondence theory of truth is false. For every version of the correspondence theory of truth should imply, at the very least, the points of agreement between Russell, Austin, and Moore. Every version should say, at least, that there is a relation of *corresponding to* holding between each truth and that which makes it true, that which it is appropriately about.[3]

---

[3] Some might object that the following theory of truth, arguably that of Wittgenstein (1961), is a version of the correspondence theory, even though the following theory denies that, in general, what it is to be true is to correspond to something. For elementary propositions, what it is to be true is to correspond to something; all other propositions are truth-functionally constructed out of elementary propositions, and so inherit their truth-values from the truth-values of their constituent elementary propositions.

I am not sure that this disjunctive account merits the name 'correspondence theory'. And whatever we call it, the account is false. Premiss: some subjunctive conditionals are true. But subjunctive conditionals are not truth-functional. So the only way this account can accommodate them is to insist that they are, contrary to appearances, elementary propositions. (For this account says that all truths are either elementary or truth-functionally constructed out of elementary propositions.) Then this account implies that each true subjunctive conditional—since it is an elementary proposition—is true in virtue of corresponding to an existing thing. We should infer from Ch. 7 that this implication is false. This

II. Realism about Truth

Consider these well-known lines from Aristotle's *Metaphysics*:
'[Thus] we define what the true and the false are. To say of
what is that it is not, or of what is not that it is, is false, while to
say of what is that it is, and of what is not that it is not, is true'
(*Metaphysics* 1011^b, 25–8 (1984: 1597)). I take Aristotle's definition
of 'the true' to be gesturing at this series of biconditionals: *that
hobbits do not exist* is true if and only if hobbits do not exist, *that
dogs bark* is true if and only if dogs bark, *that pigs fly* is true if
and only if pigs fly, and so on. Let *realism about truth* be that
series of biconditionals.

Some might complain that that series of biconditionals is
too uncontroversial to merit a lofty name like 'realism about
truth' (see Tarski 1944: 361). While I shall stick with that name,
I do agree with these complainers that realism about truth is
not controversial. Indeed, my main point in this section is that
realism is far less controversial than some suggest. In particular,
I shall oppose philosophers who think that realism—that
is, that series of biconditionals—implies the correspondence
theory of truth.

Let us begin with those philosophers who seem to take
realism to be identical with the correspondence theory. For
example, Richard Kirkham (1992: 119–20) describes the passage
from Aristotle just quoted as offering 'the first correspondence-
as-correlation theory' of truth. And A. N. Prior says: '[Moore's]
friend's belief that he has gone away is true if and only if *his
friend believes that he has*, and he has. And more generally, to
say that X's belief that *p* is true is to say that X believes that
p and (it is the case that) *p*. There seems no reason to see
any more in "correspondence with fact" than this' (1971: 22).
Perhaps Kirkham and Prior are using the expression 'the

disjunctive account of truth founders in similar ways with respect to some modal
truths (Ch. 6, §VI) and some truths about the past (Ch. 6).

correspondence theory' to mean realism about truth. If so, then they are guilty only of an infelicity. But perhaps they really are conflating (what I have called) the correspondence theory with realism about truth. If so, we can easily show that they are mistaken.[4]

Here is one way to show this. Realism insists that *that hobbits do not exist* is true if and only if hobbits do not exist. But realism does not insist—does not so much as even hint—that there is some positively existing entity that is what *that hobbits do not exist* is about, in any sense of 'about' at all, and that being appropriately related to this entity is what it is for *that hobbits do not exist* to be true. The correspondence theory of truth, however, does insist on all of this. So realism is not identical with the correspondence theory of truth.

Realism is not the correspondence theory. Nevertheless, one might argue that, even though realism is distinct from the correspondence theory, realism implies the correspondence theory. We find such an argument in G. E. Moore. Moore begins by claiming that the 'pragmatic' theory of truth, which equates truth with what is useful, is not consistent with realism about truth: '[The pragmatic theory of truth] implies that my friend's belief that I had gone away for my holidays, might be true in every sense of the word, even if I had *not* gone away: that it would be thus *true*, provided only it led up to certain kinds of satisfactory results. And similarly, of course, in millions of other instances' (1953: 282). Moore takes the pragmatic and correspondence theories to be the only live options. So he thinks that by implying the falsity of the pragmatic theory, realism implies the truth of the correspondence theory.

Here is how one objection that Russell offers to the coherence theory of truth begins: 'It may be that, with sufficient

---

[4] Alston (1996: 37–8) also seems to identify the correspondence theory with realism. Perhaps Armstrong (2004: 7) does as well, since he tells us that 'realists' should embrace Truthmaker, which he takes to be the correspondence theory (Ch. 1, §I). See also Molnar 2000: 85.

imagination, a novelist might invent a past for the world that would perfectly fit on to what we know, and yet be quite different from the real past' (1912: 122). Russell thinks that the coherence theory implies that the novelist's claims would be true, even though the world would not have been as the novelist says it was. So Russell thinks that realism rules out the coherence theory. Taking the coherence theory to be the only serious competitor to the correspondence theory, Russell then joins Moore in concluding that realism implies the correspondence theory.

I said that realism about truth is not controversial. If I am right, then defenders of the pragmatic and coherence theories of truth will want to resist these arguments by Moore and Russell. But even if Moore and Russell are correct, and the coherence and pragmatic theories are not consistent with realism, realists need not be correspondence theorists. For there are theories of truth other than those considered by Moore (1953) and Russell (1912). And some of those other theories are not only distinct from the correspondence theory, but are also consistent with realism. Any such theory—one of which is defended in § IV, another of which is opposed in § V—shows that realism about truth is not in thrall to the correspondence theory. This is good news for realists, since, as we have seen, the correspondence theory is false.

III. Coherence and Identity Theories

The first section of this chapter showed that some of the considerations that count against Truthmaker also count against the correspondence theory of truth. And this section shows that similar considerations count against two more theories of truth, the coherence theory and the identity theory. The point of this section is not, however, to discredit these two theories in particular. Rather, the point is to illustrate that some considerations that count against Truthmaker will count against every theory that takes *being true* to be a relation between a truth-bearer and an existing entity or entities.

The most natural way to read the coherence theory of truth involves actual, positively existing beliefs both as truth-bearers and as that with which such bearers cohere. Let us read the theory this way (for now). So let us take the coherence theory to say that *what it is* for a belief *b* to be true is for there to be some beliefs of an appropriate sort and number with which *b* coheres. This implies that, necessarily, *b* is true only if an appropriate number and sort of beliefs exist and cohere with *b*. Thus every truth, given the coherence theory, has a supervenience base constituted by other beliefs.[5]

Consider a possible world W_1 in which a golden mountain exists in a galaxy far from you; let us add that in that world you believe falsely that no such mountain exists. Now consider a world W_2, which lacks a golden mountain but is otherwise as much like W_1 as possible. In W_2, unlike in W_1, you truly believe that no golden mountain exists. So coherence theorists must add that W_2 has something that W_1 lacks—namely, a supervenience base, constituted only by beliefs, for the truth of your belief that a golden mountain does not exist.

I have two objections to this addition, and so two objections to the coherence theory. The first objection resembles an objection raised to Truthmaker in Chapter 4 (§I): it is not plausible that, necessarily, we can 'remove' a golden mountain only if we 'replace' it with something else.

---

[5] My argument here will not turn on any details about the nature of the coherence relation, just as the argument in the preceding section did not turn on any details about the analysis of *corresponding to*. The weakest account of coherence is mere consistency. On the other end of the spectrum, Brand Blanshard says (stunningly) that in a completely coherent system, 'No proposition would be arbitrary, every proposition would be entailed by the others jointly and even singly' (1941: 265).

A truthmaker theorist might say that annihilating the sole golden mountain necessitates that the universe exemplifies *being such that there is no golden mountain* and the existence of a resulting state of affairs. As the first objection implies, I think it is bad to say that 'removing' the mountain necessarily results in 'replacing' it with that state of affairs. But it is worse to say—as coherence theorists must—that, necessarily, to 'remove' that distant mountain is to 'replace' it with the existence of *new beliefs*. This is the second objection.[6]

These two objections take the coherence theory to say that a truth must cohere with actual beliefs. This is the simplest version of that theory. But it is not the version that coherence theorists are most likely to defend. They are likely to say, instead, that to be true is to cohere with some *hypothetical* beliefs. So the coherentist Brand Blanshard claims: 'a system of thought is true just so far as it succeeds in embodying that end which thought in its very essence is seeking to embody' (1941: 273).

Imagine someone whose beliefs enjoy 'that end which thought seeks to embody'. So she has the appropriate number of beliefs of the appropriate sort, and they cohere in just the right way. (We could even add that she lives in a coherentist utopia, all of whose citizens' belief systems are not only individually coherent, but also cohere perfectly with each other.) Her beliefs, according to the hypothetical coherence theory, would all be completely true, since being true *just is* being a part of an ideally coherent system.

Suppose that this paragon of coherence believes that there is no golden mountain. *What it is* for this belief of hers to be

---

[6] The second objection does not rely on negative existential truths. Suppose we believe falsely that dogs bark; suppose instead that dogs actually meow. Now go to a world as much like ours as possible, but in which it is true that dogs bark. The coherentist must insist, implausibly, that every such world includes, in addition to barking dogs, beliefs that constitute a supervenience base for the truth of *that dogs bark*.

true, given the hypothetical coherence theory, is for it to be related to her other beliefs in the right way. But we should deny that this negative existential is true because of how it is related to any positively existing thing or things, other beliefs included (Ch. 3, §V). Instead, we should say that it is true because there is no golden mountain. This is one reason to reject the hypothetical coherence theory; it is also, of course, a reason to reject the version of the coherence theory that invokes only actually existing beliefs.

Moreover, surely it is possible for our heroine to have just the beliefs that she has while a golden mountain—perhaps one inhabited by hobbits—exists in another solar system. Again, surely we could 'add' a golden mountain without 'subtracting from' or 'adding to' her beliefs. But the hypothetical coherence theory must deny this, at least if it is to hang on to realism about truth. This is another reason to reject the hypothetical coherence theory; and it is also, of course, another reason to reject the version of the coherence theory that invokes only actually existing beliefs.

Let us leave the coherence theory and turn to the 'identity theory of truth'. *The Stanford Encyclopedia of Philosophy* describes that theory as follows:

The simplest and most general statement of the identity theory of truth is that when a truth-bearer (e.g., a proposition) is true, there is a truth-maker (e.g., a fact) with which it is identical and the truth of the former *consists in* its identity with the latter. The theory is best understood by contrast with a rival such as the correspondence theory, according to which the relation of truth-bearer to truth-maker is correspondence rather than identity. (Candlish 2002)

In explaining and defending the identity theory, Jennifer Hornsby (1997) says that what we think, at least when we think truly, is itself 'out in the world'. Again, Hornsby says, citing John McDowell (1994) for inspiration, that what we think truly are states of affairs or facts or events. In Hornsby's words, for a 'thinkable' to be true just is for it to be identical with a 'fact'.

Hornsby's idea is not that what we normally think of as a true proposition is its own truthmaker. So her idea is not, for example, that eternally existing abstracta, abstracta that could have been false, are all their own truthmakers. Rather, her idea is that what we normally think of as a truthmaker—that is, a state of affairs or an event, or even an object like a chair or a dog—is the proposition that that truthmaker makes true. And this seems to be the idea behind all forms of the identity theory. But some truths are not made true by any event or object or anything else. Some truths lack truthmakers. Obviously enough, those truths cannot be identified with their truthmakers. So the identity theory of truth is false.

IV. Truth as a Primitive

The correspondence theory, the coherence theory, and the identity theory all purport to analyse truth as a relation between a truth-bearer and some existing entity or entities, whether those entities be states of affairs or beliefs or something else. (The hypothetical version of the coherence theory endorses such an analysis only in the ideal case.) As we saw above, one reason that all three of these theories fail is that some truths—those that lack truthmakers—are not true in virtue of how they are related to any positively existing entity or entities.

Some truths are not true in virtue of how they are related to any existing entity or entities. So we should reject any theory of truth that implies that every truth is true in virtue of how it is related to some existing entity or entities. So we should reject any theory that implies that *what it is* to be true is to be appropriately related to some existing entity or entities. And so we should reject any theory of truth that takes *being true* to be a relation between each true (primary) truth-bearer and some entity or entities. Therefore, we should conclude that *being true* is not a relation between a truth and some entity.

Being true is not a relation. One might react to this by denying that there is any property, relational or otherwise, of *being true*. I shall consider this denial in the next section. But for now, let us assume that there is a property of *being true*. Assuming this, and given that *being true* is not a relation, we have a single option. *Being true* is a monadic property.[7]

Being true is monadic. But it is not intrinsic. For whether a proposition exemplifies *being true* is often a matter of how things are around it. For example, whether *that dogs bark* is true is not only a matter of what that proposition is like, but also a matter of whether there are any dogs and what those dogs do.

Non-intrinsic monadic properties should be familiar. Both Truthmaker and TSB require (something relevantly like) the property of *being such that there is nothing more in the universe* (Ch. 3; Ch. 4, §VII). Suppose that that property were exemplified by something without proper parts. Then that property could not be a relation between what exemplifies it and something else, since, *ex hypothesi*, there is nothing else. So it would be monadic. So—if there is such a property at all—it

---

[7] More carefully, the argument just given shows that *being true* is both monadic and, moreover, is not had by a truth-bearer in virtue of that truth-bearer's standing in a relation to something else. (In this regard *being true* differs from, e.g., *being married*, which is monadic but which one has in virtue of standing in the *being married to* relation to someone else.) In what follows, when I speak of 'monadic but non-intrinsic properties', I shall mean only those properties that are not only monadic, but also not had by something in virtue of standing in a relation to something else.

My argument for the monadicity of *being true* does not rule out the possibility that *being true* is not a monadic property, but is instead a relation that holds between a proposition and itself. (The same goes for *being such that there is nothing more in the universe*, discussed below.) But I shall ignore this possibility, since I think that it makes no significant difference to the points at issue here.

is monadic. But it is not intrinsic, since whether something has that property is a matter of what (if anything) else there is.

Truthmaker and TSB imply (something like) a 'nothing more' property. Similarly, I think that every account of *being true* as a relation needs (something like) a 'nothing more' property. For every such account must deliver, for each negative existential, some entity such that that negative existential is true in virtue of how it is related to that entity. Thus any relational account of *being true*, no less than an account of *being true* as a monadic property, is committed to some non-intrinsic monadic property or other.[8]

But *being true* is monadic. Because it is monadic, if *being true* has an analysis, that analysis must be in terms of monadic properties had by each and every truth-bearer. But—here is the weak step in this argument—I do not think any monadic properties of truths deliver an analysis of *being true*.[9] So I conclude that *being true* has no analysis. That is, *being true* is a primitive property.[10]

Perhaps you have doubts about the weak step in the argument. Perhaps you think there is, or at least might be, a genuine analysis of *being true* in terms of the other monadic properties of truth-bearers. I do not want to argue about it. For the monadicity of *being true* is the main point here. Its primitivity is not essential to the other claims about truth made in this chapter or, indeed, in this book.

[8] Truthmaker, TSB, and relational accounts of *being true* can also make do with a *totalling* or *alling* relation, which is a relation that holds between entities if and only if there are no other entities in existence—so only if what is happening 'outside' those entities is a certain way. Any such relation is relevantly like a monadic but non-intrinsic property.

[9] Russell considers—just to slap away—the idea that truth could be analysed as the intrinsic 'vividness' of a belief (1912: 121).

[10] That is, the truth of primary truth-bearers is not analysable. But the truth of a derivative truth-bearer is analysed in terms of its expressing a primary truth-bearer that has the primitive property of *being true*. (And while I think that *being true* and *being false* can be 'interdefined', I deny that this gives us a genuine analysis of either.)

Nevertheless, I do think that *being true* is primitive. And others have drawn more or less the same conclusion. Here is Donald Davidson:

For the most part, the concepts philosophers single out for attention ... are the most elementary concepts we have ... Why then should we expect to be able to reduce these concepts definitionally to other concepts that are simpler, clearer, and more basic? We should accept the fact that what makes these concepts so important must also foreclose on the possibility of finding a foundation for them which reaches deeper into bedrock.

We should apply this obvious observation to the concept of truth: we cannot hope to underpin it with something more transparent or easier to grasp. Truth is, as G. E. Moore, Bertrand Russell, and Gottlob Frege maintained ... an indefinable concept. (1996: 264–265)

When he mentions Moore and Russell, Davidson cannot have in mind their correspondence theories discussed above. Instead, he must be thinking of an earlier position of theirs, defended in Moore (1899) and Russell (1904: 521–4; see also Russell 1907).[11] And with his reference to Frege, Davidson must be thinking of 'Der Gedanke', where Frege says: 'So it seems

---

[11] Russell's and Moore's position also has elements of an identity theory of truth (see Cartwright 1987; Candlish 1989). Like the identity theorist, Russell (1904) takes true propositions to be events. Unlike the identity theorist, however, Russell thinks that only those events that have the primitive property of *being true* are true (these are 'facts', in the parlance of Russell 1904). And Russell (1904) says that false propositions are events with the primitive property of *being false* (these are 'objective falsehoods').

Moore (1899: 180) takes a proposition to be a 'synthesis of concepts'. He then goes on to tell us: 'It seems necessary, then, to regard the world as formed of concepts. These are the only objects of knowledge. They cannot be regarded fundamentally as abstractions either from things or from ideas; since both alike can, if anything is to be true of them, be composed of nothing but concepts' (1899: 182; see also Moore 1901–2). I defend Russell's and Moore's view that *being true* is primitive, but of course I deny that the bearers of *being true* are events or states of affairs. Nor can I make good sense of the events that are supposed by Russell and Moore to have the property of *being false*.

likely that the content of the word "true" is *sui generis* and indefinable' (1997*b*: 327).[12]

Paul Horwich objects to the idea that *being true* is a primitive property:

there is the one-time thesis of Moore (1899 ...) and Russell (1904) that truth is an indefinable, inexplicable quality that some propositions simply have and others simply lack—a fundamental property of which no account can be provided. This gives a sense of impenetrable mysteriousness to the notion of truth and can be the resort only of those who feel that the decent alternatives have been exhausted. (1998: 9–10)

Horwich objects that if truth were not analysable, it would be mysterious.

My reply to this objection begins by noting that, even if we set *being true* aside, there are some primitive and non-analysable properties. And surely some of these are not mysterious. Moreover, if they were all mysterious, analysable properties would be equally occult, themselves ultimately analysed in terms of the inscrutable primitive properties.

Some might reply that the analysis of non-primitive properties never bottoms out in primitive properties, but rather descends through other analysable properties *ad infinitum*. Taking this option into account—and assuming that not every property is mysterious—we must say at least one of two things. First, some non-mysterious properties have no analysis. Second, some non-mysterious properties have an infinitely complex analysis.

---

[12] But note: 'The *Bedeutung* of the word 'true' seems altogether *sui generis*. May we not be dealing here with something which cannot be called a property in the ordinary sense at all? In spite of this doubt, I will begin by expressing myself in accordance with ordinary usage, as if truth were a property, until some more appropriate way of speaking is found' (Frege 1997*b*: 328–9). It is hard to square these claims with Frege's earlier and better-known discussion of truth in 'Über Sinn und Bedeutung', in which he claims that truth, or at least the True, is the referent of each and every true sentence (see Frege 1997*a*: 157–8).

I endorse the first: among the non-mysterious properties are some that are primitive. This is partly because if a property had an infinitely complex analysis, an analysis that we could not possibly grasp, that property would seem to be mysterious. And it is partly because we obviously do grasp certain primitive properties. Among these are *identity*, *existence*, and—as was suggested at the end of Chapter 5—some modal properties.[13]

Focus on *identity*. The received view about *identity* is that it is primitive and cannot be analysed into more fundamental relations or properties (see Merricks 1998: 110; Hawthorne 2003: 99). The received view does not monger mystery. For even if identity is primitive, we know a lot about it. We know, for example, that it is transitive, reflexive, and symmetric, and also that it implies indiscernibility. And we can even make claims of identity in English without using the word 'identity'. For example, we can say that x is one and the same as y.

Similarly, the primitive nature of *being true* is consistent with our knowing a lot about truth. It is consistent with our knowing that, necessarily, *that hobbits do not exist* has the property of *being true* if and only if there are no hobbits; more generally, it is consistent with our knowing that realism about truth is correct. Similarly, it is consistent with truth's depending on being in a trivial and uncontroversial way. That is, even if *being true* is

---

[13] Grasping primitive properties is more problematic than grasping properties generally only if the only way to grasp a property is by grasping its analysis. (Obviously, we do not grasp primitive properties by grasping their analyses; they have no analyses.) But it is false that the only way to grasp a property is by grasping its analysis. To see this, consider that either some of the properties we grasp are analysed in terms of primitive properties, or none is. If some are, then to grasp their analysis requires grasping primitive properties—but that cannot be done if the only way to grasp a property is to grasp its analysis. If none is, then to grasp the analysis of a property requires grasping an infinitely complex and unending analysis—but that is not something we can do. So I conclude that at least some properties can be grasped even if we do not grasp their analyses. Further support for this conclusion comes from the observation that few properties have uncontroversial analyses; so, if to grasp a property always required grasping its analysis, we would grasp far fewer properties than we actually do grasp.

primitive, *that hobbits do not exist* is true because hobbits do not exist. More generally, the many claims about truth defended throughout this book, along with the arguments in support of them, are consistent with *being true*'s being primitive. And we can, while speaking English, assert that a statement is true without using the word 'true'. For example, we can say that a particular statement tells it like it is.

Being true is primitive. This does not render truth mysterious. Moreover, I think that a primitive property of *being true* is preferable to the primitive properties implied by Truthmaker, TSB, and relational theories of *being true*. That is, a primitive (and monadic and non-intrinsic) *being true* is preferable to primitive (and monadic and non-intrinsic) properties like *being such that there is nothing more in the universe*.

V. There is a Property of *Being True*

'Deflationism' about truth can be understood in a number of ways. For example, it might be understood as the claim that truth cannot be substantively analysed. Thus understood, the view that *being true* is primitive counts as deflationist (see Stoljar 1997). But I am not going to understand deflationism in this way, or in any of a number of other legitimate ways. Instead, I shall take 'deflationism' to be nothing other than the claim that there is no property of *being true*.

Deflationism, as I here understand it, is consistent with my argument above for the claim that *being true* is not a relation. It is also consistent with my claim that *being true* is not analysed in terms of the monadic properties of truth-bearers. More generally, deflationists can affirm much of what I defend in this book.[14] But deflationism threatens my conclusion that *being true*

---

[14] A truthmaker for *p* is essentially such that *p* is true. I think that deflationists can accommodate truthmaking, even while denying that there is a property of

is monadic and primitive. For deflationism provides a consistent way to reject that conclusion while accepting what motivated it.

I shall respond to this threat only partially. For I shall focus on only one version of deflationism, a version inspired by Horwich's Minimal Theory of truth. I restrict my focus in this way for two reasons. First, this version of deflationism allows for truths to be abstract propositions, and is thus preferable to at least those forms of deflationism, such as prosententialism (Grover, Camp, and Belnap 1975) and disquotationalism (Quine 1986: 12), that seem to imply that all truths are sentences of some sort.

Second, Horwich opposes all general positive claims about truth's nature, even claims of the sort that some deflationists make. (Horwich will not say, for example, that truth is disquotation.) In this way, my claim that *being true* is primitive resembles Horwich's theory. Because of this, I think it is important to be explicit about the ways in which my view differs from a version of deflationism inspired by Horwich's view.

Here is Horwich's Minimal Theory (MT).

… in order for the truth predicate to fulfil its function we must acknowledge that

> (MT) The proposition *that quarks really exist* is true if and only if quarks really exist, the proposition *that lying is bad* is true if and only if lying is bad, … and so on,

but nothing more about truth need be assumed. The entire conceptual and theoretical role of truth may be explained on this basis. This confirms our suspicion that the traditional attempt to discern the *essence* of truth—to analyze that special quality which all truths supposedly have in common—is just a pseudo-problem based on syntactic overgeneralization. Unlike most other properties, *being true* is unsusceptible to conceptual or scientific analysis. No wonder that its 'underlying nature' has so stubbornly resisted philosophical elaboration; for there is simply no such thing. (Horwich 1998: 5)

---

being true. They can say, e.g., that *x* is a truthmaker for *that hobbits do not exist* only if *x* is essentially such that there are no hobbits. Similarly, I think they can accommodate TSB.

Horwich's MT does not include the claim that there is no property of *being true*. In fact, Horwich (1998: 141–4) explicitly says that, at least given some understandings of 'property', there is such a property. But I shall now build into MT the claim that there is no property of *being true*. For only given that claim is MT 'deflationist' in my sense, and so only given that claim does MT threaten my argument for the conclusion that *being true* is a primitive monadic property.

Besides, despite his claims to the contrary, Horwich should deny that there is a property of *being true*. For Horwich says, in the passage just quoted, that '*being true* is unsusceptible to conceptual or scientific analysis' (see also Horwich 1998: 138). But as we saw in the preceding section, Horwich denies that *being true* is primitive. The only way to render these two claims consistent is to deny that there is any such property at all. For only then can it be both false that *being true* is analysable and also false that *being true* is primitive.

I say that *being true* is a primitive monadic property. I shall make two points in favour of my view over the deflationist version of MT. The first point begins by reminding us that, as we saw in the last section, my view does not render truth mysterious. But, so I shall now argue, MT saddles truth, or at least our understanding of truth, with unacceptable mystery.

For starters, consider that understanding MT had better not be a matter of being able to articulate it in full. For, as Horwich himself says, 'we can't formulate MT explicitly because there are too many axioms' (1998: 11). Nevertheless, we do know how to 'go on' with respect to MT. We know to add that the proposition *that dogs bark* is true if and only if dogs bark. And we know better than to add that the proposition *that pigs fly* is true if and only if pigs walk. And so on.[15] I think that our being able to 'go on' in this way counts as our understanding MT.

---

[15] We may not know how to go on with respect to *that this proposition is false*.

But there is a problem. Given MT, it is mysterious that we know to add that *that dogs bark* is true if and only if dogs bark. More generally, it is mysterious that we know how to 'go on' adding the biconditionals that constitute MT. In particular, if MT is right, we cannot explain our ability to 'go on' by way of our understanding MT. That 'explanation' is viciously circular, since to understand MT just is to be able to 'go on'.

Nor can our ability to 'go on' be explained by our understanding truth. For, by MT's lights, there is nothing more to understanding truth than understanding MT. Thus an explanation our ability to 'go on' with respect to MT by way of our understanding truth is no less circular than an explanation by way of our understanding MT. In sum, if MT were correct, our understanding of truth would be utterly mysterious.

My own view does not have this problem. I deny that MT is all there is to say about truth. To repeat a claim from the preceding section, I say that we grasp the property of *being true*. This allows us to recognize some of what *being true* implies. (Compare: because I grasp *identity*, I recognize that it implies indiscernibility.) Among its implications are the biconditionals included in MT, some of which we understand and can articulate. Moreover, I would add, these implications play an indispensable role in our knowing which propositions are true. For example, I know that humans exist, and I know that *that humans exist* is true if and only if humans exist; this is how I know that the proposition *that humans exist* exemplifies the property of *being true*. This concludes my defence of the first point in favour of my view over MT.

Horwich thinks that one advantage of MT is that it can explain (what I have called) realism about truth. For realism is just the long series of biconditionals affirmed by MT. MT itself is simply realism plus the claim that there is nothing more to truth. And so, Horwich (1998: 11–12) says, MT's being the correct theory of truth explains why realism is correct.

But I reply that, rather than giving realism a sure footing on a theory of truth, MT renders realism, or at least our understanding of realism, mysterious. Given MT as the whole story on truth, it is mysterious that we are able to 'go on' articulating realism, for just the same reason that it is mysterious that we are able to 'go on' articulating MT itself. Unlike the defender of MT, I can that say that our ability to continue to articulate the biconditionals that constitute realism is rooted in our grasp of the property of *being true*. Thus a second point in favour of my view, over MT, is that it provides a better home for realism about truth.

REFERENCES

ADAMS, ROBERT M. (1974), 'Theories of Actuality', *Noûs*, 8: 211–31.

—— (1987), 'Middle Knowledge and the Problem of Evil', in *The Virtue of Faith and Other Essays in Philosophical Theology* (New York: Oxford University Press). Original version published in *American Philosophical Quarterly*, 14 (1977): 109–17.

ALSTON, WILLIAM P. (1996), *A Realist Conception of Truth* (Ithaca, NY: Cornell University Press).

ARISTOTLE (1984), *The Complete Works of Aristotle: The Revised Oxford Translation*, i–ii, ed. Jonathan Barnes (Princeton: Princeton University Press).

ARMSTRONG, D. M. (1978), *Nominalism and Realism: Universals and Scientific Realism*, i (Cambridge: Cambridge University Press).

—— (1989a), 'C. B. Martin, Counterfactuals, Causality, and Conditionals', in John Heil (ed.), *Cause, Mind, and Reality: Essays Honouring C. B. Martin* (Dordrecht: Kluwer).

—— (1989b), *Universals: An Opinionated Introduction* (Boulder, Colo.: Westview Press).

—— (1997), *A World of States of Affairs* (Cambridge: Cambridge University Press).

—— (2000), 'Difficult Cases in the Theory of Truthmaking', *The Monist*, 83: 150–60.

—— (2003), 'Truthmakers for Modal Truths', in Hallvard Lillehammer and Gonzalo Rodriguez-Pereya (eds.), *Real Metaphysics* (London: Routledge).

—— (2004), *Truth and Truthmakers* (Cambridge: Cambridge University Press).

AUSTIN, J. L. (1979), 'Truth', in *Philosophical Papers*, 3rd edn. (Oxford: Oxford University Press). Originally published in *Proceedings of the Aristotelian Society*, suppl. vol. 24 (1950): 111–29.

BALASHOV, YURI, and JANSSEN, MICHEL (2003), 'Critical Notice: Presentism and Relativity', *British Journal for the Philosophy of Science*, 54: 327–46.

BEEBEE, HELEN, and DODD, JULIAN (2005), 'Introduction', in *Truth-makers: The Contemporary Debate* (Oxford: Clarendon Press).

BERGMANN, MICHAEL (1999), '(Serious) Actualism and (Serious) Presentism', *Noûs*, 33: 118–32.

BERTOLET, ROD (1993), 'Hasker on Middle Knowledge', *Faith and Philosophy*, 10: 3–17.

BIGELOW, JOHN (1988), *The Reality of Numbers: A Physicalist's Philosophy of Mathematics* (Oxford: Clarendon Press).

——(1996), 'Presentism and Properties', in James E. Tomberlin (ed.), *Philosophical Perspectives, x: Metaphysics* (Oxford: Blackwell Publishers).

BLANSHARD, BRAND (1941), *The Nature of Thought*, ii (New York: The Macmillan Company).

CANDLISH, STEWART (1989), 'The Truth about F. H. Bradley', *Mind*, 98: 331–48.

——(2002), 'The Identity Theory of Truth', *Stanford Encyclopedia of Philosophy* (plato.stanford.edu).

CARTWRIGHT, RICHARD (1987), 'A Neglected Theory of Truth', in *Philosophical Essays* (Cambridge, Mass.: MIT Press).

CHISHOLM, RODERICK M. (1976), *Person and Object* (LaSalle, Ill.: Open Court Publishing Co.).

——(1990), 'Entities without Times: An Essay on Ontology', *Noûs*, 24: 413–28.

CRAIG, WILLIAM LANE (2001), 'Middle-Knowledge, Truth-makers, and the "Grounding Objection"', *Faith and Philosophy*, 18: 337–52.

CRESSWELL, M. J. (1990), *Entities and Indices* (Dordrecht: Kluwer Academic Publishers).

CRISP, THOMAS (2003), 'Presentism', in Michael J. Loux and Dean Zimmerman (eds.), *The Oxford Handbook of Metaphysics* (Oxford: Oxford University Press).

——(2004), 'On Presentism and Triviality' and 'Reply to Ludlow', in Dean Zimmerman (ed.), *Oxford Studies in Metaphysics*, i (Oxford: Clarendon Press).

——(2007), 'Presentism and the Grounding Objection', *Noûs* (forthcoming).

DAVIDSON, DONALD (1996), 'The Folly of Trying to Define Truth', *Journal of Philosophy*, 93: 263–78.

DODD, JULIAN (2002), 'Is Truth Supervenient on Being?', *Proceedings of the Aristotelian Society*, 102: 69–86.

DUMMETT, MICHAEL (1978), 'The Reality of the Past', in *Truth and Other Enigmas* (Cambridge, Mass.: Harvard University Press).

Originally published in *Proceedings of the Aristotelian Society*, 69 (1969): 239–58.

FINE, KIT (1982), 'First-Order Modal Theories III—Facts', *Synthese*, 53: 43–122.

FLINT, THOMAS P. (1998), *Divine Providence: The Molinist Account* (Ithaca, NY: Cornell University Press).

FOX, JOHN F. (1987), 'Truthmaker', *Australasian Journal of Philosophy*, 65: 188–207.

FREDDOSO, ALFRED J. (1988), 'Introduction', in Molina's *On Divine Foreknowledge: Part IV of the Concordia* (Ithaca, NY: Cornell University Press).

FREGE, GOTTLOB (1997a), 'On *Sinn* and *Bedeutung*', in Michael Beaney (ed.), *The Frege Reader* (Oxford: Blackwell Publishing Ltd.). Originally published in *Zeitschrift für Philosophie und philosophische Kritik*, 100 (1892): 25–50.

—— (1997b), 'Thought [*Der Gedanke*]', in Michael Beaney (ed.), *The Frege Reader* (Oxford: Blackwell Publishing Ltd.). Originally published in *Beiträge zur Philosophie des deutschen Idealismus*, I (1918–19): 58–77.

GROVER, DOROTHY L.; CAMP, JOSEPH L.; and BELNAP JR., NUEL D. (1975), 'A Prosentential Theory of Truth', *Philosophical Studies*, 27: 73–125.

HASKER, WILLIAM (1986), 'A Refutation of Middle Knowledge', *Noûs*, 20: 545–57.

—— (1989), *God, Time, and Knowledge* (Ithaca, NY: Cornell University Press).

HAWLEY, KATHERINE (2001), *How Things Persist* (Oxford: Clarendon Press).

HAWTHORNE, JOHN (2003), 'Identity', in Michael J. Loux and Dean Zimmerman (eds.), *The Oxford Handbook of Metaphysics* (Oxford: Oxford University Press).

HAZEN, ALLEN (1976), 'Expressive Completeness in Modal Language', *Journal of Philosophical Logic*, 5: 25–46.

—— (1979), 'Counterpart-Theoretic Semantics for Modal Logic', *Journal of Philosophy*, 76: 319–38.

HEIL, JOHN (2004), 'Properties and Powers', in Dean Zimmerman (ed.), *Oxford Studies in Metaphysics*, i (Oxford: Clarendon Press).

HELLER, MARK (1998), 'Property Counterparts in Ersatz Worlds', *Journal of Philosophy*, 95: 293–316.

HINCHLIFF, MARK (1996), 'The Puzzle of Change', in James E. Tomberlin (ed.), *Philosophical Perspectives, x: Metaphysics* (Oxford: Blackwell Publishers).

HORNSBY, JENNIFER (1997), 'Truth: The Identity Theory', *Proceedings of the Aristotelian Society*, 97: 1–24.

HORWICH, PAUL (1998), *Truth*, 2nd edn. (Oxford: Clarendon Press).

HUDSON, HUD (1997), 'Brute Facts', *Australasian Journal of Philosophy*, 75: 77–82.

JACKSON, FRANK (1994), 'Armchair Metaphysics' in Michaelis Michael and John O'Leary-Hawthorne (eds.), *Philosophy in Mind: The Place of Philosophy in the Study of Mind* (Dordrecht: Kluwer Academic Publishers).

KELLER, SIMON (2004), 'Presentism and Truthmaking', in Dean Zimmerman (ed.), *Oxford Studies in Metaphysics*, i (Oxford: Clarendon Press).

KIRKHAM, RICHARD H. (1992), *Theories of Truth: A Critical Introduction* (Cambridge, Mass.: MIT Press).

KRIPKE, SAUL (1980), *Naming and Necessity* (Cambridge, Mass.: Harvard University Press).

LEWIS, DAVID (1986), *On the Plurality of Worlds* (Oxford: Basil Blackwell, Ltd.).

—— (1999a), 'Armstrong on Combinatorial Possibility', in *Papers on Metaphysics and Epistemology* (Cambridge: Cambridge University Press). Originally published in *Australasian Journal of Philosophy*, 70 (1992): 211–24.

—— (1999b), 'Finkish Dispositions', in *Papers on Metaphysics and Epistemology* (Cambridge: Cambridge University Press). Originally published in *Philosophical Quarterly*, 47 (1997): 143–58.

—— (2001), 'Truthmaking and Difference-Making', *Noûs*, 35: 602–15.

—— (2003), 'Things qua Truthmakers', in Hallvard Lillehammer and Gonzalo Rodriguez-Pereya (eds.), *Real Metaphysics* (London: Routledge).

—— (2004), 'Tensed Quantifiers', in Dean Zimmerman (ed.), *Oxford Studies in Metaphysics*, i (Oxford: Clarendon Press).

LOMBARD, LAWRENCE BRIAN (1999), 'On the Alleged Incompatibility of Presentism and Temporal Parts', *Philosophia*, 27: 253–60.

LOWE, E. J. (1998), *The Possibility of Metaphysics: Substance, Identity, and Time* (Oxford: Clarendon Press).

LUCRETIUS (1994), *On the Nature of the Universe*, trans. R. E. Latham; rev. John Godwin (London: Penguin Books Ltd.).

LUKASIEWICZ, JAN (1967), 'On Determinism', in Storrs McCall (ed.), *Polish Logic: 1920–1939* (Oxford: Clarendon Press).

MACKIE, J. L. (1977), *Ethics: Inventing Right and Wrong* (London: Pelican Books).

MARKOSIAN, NED (1995), 'The Open Past', *Philosophical Studies*, 79: 95–105.

—— (2004), 'A Defense of Presentism', in Dean Zimmerman (ed.), *Oxford Studies in Metaphysics*, i (Oxford: Clarendon Press).

MARTIN, C. B. (1993), 'Power for Realists', in John Bacon, Keith Campbell, and Lloyd Reinhart (eds.), *Ontology, Causality, and Mind: Essays in Honour of D. M. Armstrong* (Cambridge: Cambridge University Press).

—— (1994), 'Dispositions and Conditionals', *Philosophical Quarterly*, 44: 1–8.

—— (1996), 'How It Is: Entities, Absences, and Voids', *Australasian Journal of Philosophy*, 74: 57–65.

McGRATH, MATTHEW (1997), 'Weak Deflationism', *Mind*, 106: 69–98.

—— (2003), 'What the Deflationist May Say about Truthmaking', *Philosophy and Phenomenological Research*, 66: 666–88.

McDOWELL, JOHN (1994), *Mind and World* (Cambridge, Mass.: Harvard University Press).

MERRICKS, TRENTON (1994), 'Endurance and Indiscernibility', *Journal of Philosophy*, 91: 165–84.

—— (1995), 'On the Incompatibility of Enduring and Perduring Entities', *Mind*, 104: 523–31.

—— (1998), 'There Are No Criteria of Identity over Time', *Noûs*, 32: 106–24.

—— (1999), 'Persistence, Parts, and Presentism', *Noûs*, 33: 421–38.

—— (2001), *Objects and Persons* (Oxford: Clarendon Press).

—— (2003*a*), 'The End of Counterpart Theory', *Journal of Philosophy*, 100: 521–49.

—— (2003*b*), 'Maximality and Consciousness', *Philosophy and Phenomenological Research*, 66: 150–58.

—— (2003*c*), 'Review of *How Things Persist*', *Mind*, 112: 146–48.

—— (2005), 'Composition and Vagueness', *Mind*, 114: 615–37.

—— (2006), 'Good-Bye Growing Block', in Dean Zimmerman (ed.), *Oxford Studies in Metaphysics*, ii (Oxford: Clarendon Press).

MOLINA, LUIS DE (1988), *On Divine Foreknowledge: Part IV of the Concordia*, trans. Alfred J. Freddoso (Ithaca, NY: Cornell University Press.)

MOLNAR, GEORGE (2000), 'Truthmakers for Negative Truths', *Australasian Journal of Philosophy*, 78: 72–86.

—— (2003), *Powers: A Study in Metaphysics* (Oxford: Oxford University Press).

MOORE, G. E. (1899), 'The Nature of Judgment', *Mind*, 8: 176–93.

—— (1901–2), 'Truth', in J. Baldwin (ed.), *Dictionary of Philosophy and Psychology* (London: MacMillan).

—— (1903), *Principia Ethica* (Cambridge: Cambridge University Press).

—— (1953), *Some Main Problems of Philosophy* (London: George Allen & Unwin Ltd.).

MULLIGAN, KEVIN; SIMONS, PETER; and SMITH, BARRY (1984), 'Truth-Makers', *Philosophy and Phenomenological Research*, 44: 287–321.

OLIVER, ALEX (1996), 'The Metaphysics of Properties', *Mind*, 105: 1–80.

OLSON, ERIC (1997), *The Human Animal: Personal Identity without Psychology* (Oxford: Oxford University Press).

OTTE, RICHARD (1987), 'A Defense of Middle Knowledge', *International Journal for Philosophy of Religion*, 21: 161–69.

PLANTINGA, ALVIN (1974), *The Nature of Necessity* (Oxford: Clarendon Press).

—— (1985), 'Self-Profile' and 'Replies', in James E. Tomberlin and Peter van Inwagen (eds.), *Alvin Plantinga* (Dordrecht: D. Reidel).

—— (1987), 'Two Concepts of Modality: Modal Realism and Modal Reductionism', in James E. Tomberlin (ed.), *Philosophical Perspectives, i: Metaphysics* (Atascadero, Calif.: Ridgeview Publishing Co.).

PRIOR, A. N. (1968), 'Changes in Events and Changes in Things', in *Papers in Time and Tense* (Oxford: Oxford University Press).

—— (1971), *Objects of Thought* (Oxford: Clarendon Press).

QUINE, W. V. O. (1960), *Word and Object* (Cambridge, Mass.: MIT Press).

—— (1966), 'Necessary Truth', in *The Ways of Paradox and Other Essays* (Cambridge, Mass.: Harvard University Press).

—— (1969), 'Propositional Objects', in *Ontological Relativity and Other Essays* (New York: Columbia University Press).

—— (1974), *The Roots of Reference* (LaSalle, Ill.: Open Court Publishing Co.).

—— (1986), *Philosophy of Logic*, 2nd edn. (Cambridge, Mass.: Harvard University Press).

REA, MICHAEL C. (2003), 'Four-Dimensionalism', in Michael J. Loux and Dean Zimmerman (eds.), *The Oxford Handbook of Metaphysics* (Oxford: Oxford University Press).

RESTALL, GREG (1996), 'Truthmakers, Entailment, and Necessity', *Australasian Journal of Philosophy*, 74: 331–40.

RHODA, ALAN R; BOYD, GREGORY A.; and BELT, THOMAS G. (forthcoming), 'Open Theism, Omniscience, and the Nature of the Future', *Faith and Philosophy*.

ROSEN, GIDEON (1990), 'Modal Fictionalism', *Mind*, 99: 327–54.

RUSSELL, BERTRAND (1904), 'Meinong's Theory of Complexes and Assumptions', *Mind*, 13: 204–19, 336–54, and 509–24.

——— (1907), 'On the Nature of Truth', *Proceedings of the Aristotelian Society*, 2: 28–49.

——— (1912), *The Problems of Philosophy* (London: Williams & Norgate).

——— (1919), 'Propositions: What They Are and How They Mean', *Proceedings of the Aristotelian Society*, suppl. vol. 2: 1–43.

——— (1940), *An Inquiry into Meaning and Truth* (London: George Allen & Unwin Ltd.).

——— (1985), *The Philosophy of Logical Atomism*, ed. David Pears (Chicago: Open Court Publishing). Originally published in *The Monist*, 28 (1918): 495–527; 29 (1919): 32–63, 190–222, and 345–80.

RYLE, GILBERT (1949), *The Concept of Mind* (Chicago: University of Chicago Press).

SHORTER, J. M. (1962), 'Facts, Logical Atomism, and Reducibility', *Australasian Journal of Philosophy*, 40: 283–302.

SIDER, THEODORE (1996), 'All the World's a Stage', *Australasian Journal of Philosophy*, 74: 433–53.

——— (1997), 'Four-Dimensionalism', *Philosophical Review*, 106: 197–231.

——— (1999), 'Presentism and Ontological Commitment', *Journal of Philosophy*, 7: 325–47.

——— (2001), *Four-Dimensionalism: An Ontology of Persistence and Time* (Oxford: Clarendon Press).

——— (2002), 'The Ersatz Pluriverse', *Journal of Philosophy*, 99: 279–315.

——— (2003), 'Reductive Theories of Modality', in Michael J. Loux and Dean Zimmerman (eds.), *The Oxford Handbook of Metaphysics* (Oxford: Oxford University Press).

——— (2006), 'Quantifiers and Temporal Ontology', *Mind*, 115: 75–97.

SMITH, BARRY (1999), 'Truthmaker Realism', *Australasian Journal of Philosophy*, 77: 274–91.

SORENSEN, ROY (2001), *Vagueness and Contradiction* (Oxford: Clarendon Press).

STOLJAR, DANIEL (1997), 'The Deflationary Theory of Truth', *Stanford Encyclopedia of Philosophy* (plato.stanford.edu).

TARSKI, ALFRED (1944), 'The Semantic Conception of Truth and the Foundations of Semantics', *Philosophy and Phenomenological Research*, 4: 341–76.

TONER, PATRICK (2006), 'Meta-ontology and Accidental Unity', *Philosophical Quarterly*, 56: 550–61.

TOOLEY, MICHAEL (1997), *Time, Tense, and Causation* (Oxford: Clarendon Press).

VAN INWAGEN, PETER (1985), 'Plantinga on Trans-World Identity', in James E. Tomberlin and Peter van Inwagen (eds.), *Alvin Plantinga* (Dordrecht: D. Reidel).

—— (1986), 'Two Concepts of Possible Worlds', *Midwest Studies in Philosophy*, 11: 185–213.

WITTGENSTEIN, LUDWIG (1961), *Tractatus Logico-Philosophicus*, trans. D. F. Pears and B. F. McGuinness (London: Routledge). Originally published in 1921 in the periodical *Annalen der Naturphilosophie*.

INDEX